Les Costello

Charlie Angus

Les Costello
Canada's Flying Father

NOVALIS

© 2005 Novalis, Saint Paul University, Ottawa, Canada

Cover design: Renée Longtin
Cover images: background – Les Costello plays for the Toronto Maple Leafs (Photo is from the Imperial Oil–Turofsky/Hockey Hall of Fame collection and is courtesy of the Hockey Hall of Fame, Toronto, www.hhof.com.) inset – Father Les Costello (Photo courtesy of Mrs. Rita [Costello] Hogan.)
Layout: Christiane Lemire

Business Office:
Novalis
49 Front Street East, 2nd Floor
Toronto, Ontario, Canada
M5E 1B3

Phone: 1-800-387-7164
Fax: (514) 278-3030
E-mail: cservice@novalis-inc.com
www.novalis.ca

Library and Archives Canada Cataloguing in Publication

Angus, Charlie
    Les Costello : Canada's flying father / Charlie Angus.

ISBN 2-89507-631-6

    1. Costello, Les, 1928–2002. 2. Priests–Ontario,
Northern–Biography.
3. Catholic Church–Canada–Clergy–Biography. 4. Flying Fathers (Hockey team) 5. Charity hockey tournaments–Canada. 6. Hockey players–Canada–Biography. 7. Ontario, Northern–Biography. 8. South Porcupine (Timmins, Ont.)–Biography. I. Title.

BX4705.C684A54 2005   282'.092   C2005-901093-2

Printed in Canada.

We acknowledge the financial support of the Government of Canada through the Book Publishing Industry Development Program (BPIDP) for our publishing activities.

5 4 3 2 1   09 08 07 06 05

Contents

Introduction 9

I. A Kid from the Porcupine
1. The Irish 14
2. A Child Is Born 18
3. The Game 25
4. A Church on Skates 32
5. Lord Stanley's Ring 42
6. The Summer of '50 48
7. The Door Swings Both Ways 54

II: God's Favourite Rebel
8. On the Mile of Gold 64
9. The Noranda Alouettes 71
10. The Flying Fathers 79
11. In the Land of Silver 86
12. A Priest and the Sacraments 94
13. St. Martin of Schumacher 105
14. The Face of Christ 112
15. A World in Change 121
16. Pulling the Goalie 132

Epilogue 139
Notes 143
Bibliography 148

To Brit, Mariah, Siobhan and Lola
for always being willing to listen to the stories

Introduction

E ver since I can remember, trading Father Costello stories has been a favourite pastime for people in my home region of northern Ontario. In some ways this is no surprise, as Costello's life was the stuff of legend. He was a hockey hero who played on four championship teams and bagged a Stanley Cup by the age of twenty. In leaving the Maple Leafs for the seeming anonymity of the role of small-town parish priest, Costello walked away from the Canadian dream. In the end, however, he achieved a level of fame that far surpassed anything he had accomplished in his pro hockey career. Costello became an instantly recognizable national and, indeed, international figure as a leader of the Flying Fathers hockey team – a group of zany priests who played a great game while raising millions for various charities. Not that any of this recognition mattered to Costello. He was continually giving the bum's rush to media, documentary makers and even Hollywood moguls interested in profiling his life. Among my own many memorable meetings with Costello were a number of failed attempts to coax an interview out of him.

Costello's home constituency – blue-collar families of the north – shared, to some extent, his disregard for his "glory years" in hockey. To these people, his hockey personality always came a distant second to his work as a priest, as seen in the rich oral lore surrounding Costello. Anyone who could tell one Costello tale was usually good for at least two or three zingers. The best stories centre on Costello's punchline at so-and-so's funeral, or the way he helped whatchamacallit's family in hard times. In story, he appears in a number of different guises: he's a rambunctious R.P. McMurphy, Ken Kesey's rebel hero in *One Flew Over the Cuckoo's Nest*, betting on the horses and driving around town in a beat-up old pickup truck; he's a northern Mother Teresa willing to give the clothes off his back for the poor.

There is, I suppose, a seeming inconsistency in these tales – a man both profane and profound. Costello could swear a blue streak, and some of that language appears from time to time in this book when I quote him. To those telling the Costello tales, however, these inconsistencies are not problematic. Oral culture simply has greater latitude for integrating the contrary strands of a man's life. In telling a tale we conjure something of a person's spirit.

This book is my attempt to capture something of the Costello spirit. But in looking at his life it becomes clear that this is not simply the story of a colourful maverick. Les Costello was very much a product of a particular culture of working-class Catholic Canadian identity. The story of his life is a cultural journey through some of the best and some of the hardest years of twentieth-century Catholicism.

* * *

Since Costello's death in December 2002, his legend has undergone a subtle but profound shift. People tell these stories as if they were hallowed relics of a better time. Certainly, death has a way of freeze-framing life and then slowly replacing some of the more garish colours with a softer sepia hue. But the shift in emphasis is also attributable to the fact that Costello's death came at a time of crisis in cultural and religious identity.

Vocations are drying up. Church pews are bereft of the young. Trust in the priesthood is at an all-time low. In the north, dynamic parishes are being shut down and their assets sold. This crisis of religious confidence is reflected in the corresponding cultural insecurity in the northern mining belt. A culture that prided itself on its "give 'em hell" zest for life has been drained by the relentless bleed-off of the young to the urban centres of the south.

Amidst this cultural and religious uncertainty, Costello personifies something we fear may be slipping away. In story he remains the undaunted rebel in a frontier land that has become tame; he's the self-sacrificing hockey hero when our own hockey heroes have become self-serving millionaires; he's the priest who opens wide the arms of comfort while the Church appears increasingly exclusive and rigid.

Unless these stories are placed in the larger context of ongoing cultural, religious and social transformation, however, the real significance of Costello's life could be lost.

"Don't call me a saint; I don't want to be dismissed that easily." So said Catholic Worker foundress Dorothy Day. Both Day and Costello were great believers in the tradition of the saints. But both were wary of the tendency to canonize their efforts because it allowed people to think that living the gospel was somehow beyond the capacity (and hence the responsibility) of "average" folk.

Costello personified a Church that was much bigger and more inclusive than anything that could be contained within the walls of a mere parish. The outpouring of grief following his death showed the broad extent of Costello's spiritual "parishioners." People identified with the man who made it seem that if a foul-talking, card-playing rabble-rouser could be a follower of Christ, so could they. It would be a shame if our homemade hagiographies reduced him to little more than a stained-glass figure. In doing so, we would lose sight of the fact that, as Father Costello used to say, God loves the rebel.

"The wind blew
and the shit flew
and in walked Les Costello...."

11

I. A Kid from the Porcupine

"Cossie came from a poor family in a small town. He was given the ability to play a rough sport. He had to work as hard as anybody else. He kicked the shit out of his opponents because that's how the game was played."

– Pat Hannigan, former NHL player

1. The Irish

"I remember Father Les and Father O'Connor coming over to my parents' place when I was young. My dad was a singer and they'd smoke cigars and listen to those sad, sad Irish songs. A little bit of drink and the emotions would flow. There were always lots of stories to be told in between the songs."

—D'Arcy Quinn, teammate on the Flying Fathers

His eye may never see the blue
of Ireland's April sky
His ear may never listen to
the song of lark on high
But deep within his Irish heart
are cloisters dim and dark
No human hand can wrench apart
And the lark still sings for him.

—"We're Irish Yet" by Henri Drummond
died, Cobalt, Ontario, 1907

T hey called themselves "the Irish," not that any of them had ever seen Erin. Ireland was a fable preserved in nighttime tales and maudlin songs. The stories had been brought off the famine ships at Quebec City in the 1800s and carried by their grandparents as they worked their way down through the lumber shanties of the St. Lawrence and lower Ottawa rivers.

For the children of the Irish diaspora, the stories spoke to something deeper than kitchen-table entertainment. The memory of the place these people had never seen anchored a collective identity: remember where your people are from and you will know who you are.

And each generation growing up in the rolling hills of the Ottawa Valley learned the lessons. They stuck together. They were clannish. They held their own amidst a sea of hostile Protestant Orange farmers on the Ontario side of the river while fighting for every job and opportunity against the equally poor French families on the Quebec side. This is the way it had been since the days of the "Shiners" – the Irish navvies who controlled the work contracts on the Rideau Canal with pickaxes and fists.

But the real mark of the Irish was their magnificent breadth of spirit. The tales instilled in these poor people a richness of the tongue and a belief that nothing on this earth was as it seemed. Thus no death could properly be mourned unless the halls rang with laughter. No humour could stand on its own without an understanding that the spirits, the little people and the saints were listening. The outsiders recognized these dualities. They called them the "Lace Curtain" Irish – a people who would seemingly open their hearts to the world, while carefully keeping their inner lives and relations hidden from view.

Just as in Ireland, the farms of the Valley proved too poor to support the large families that settled there. Each new generation experienced the bitter tang of seeing their young men leave the farms in search of work. And so, the old stories of exile, loss and remembrance became the planted perennials of settlements like Killaloe, Eganville and Fort-Coulonge.

This inner emigration had begun back in the 1850s as the Irish work crews joined the square timber flotillas on the Gatineau River in the east or through the hinterlands of Timiskaming and Mattawa in the west. When they had depleted the great White Pines for the British navy ships, the men joined the logging shanties – pushing steadily northward as the frontline troops of the great Valley lumber dynasties of Booth, Klock and O'Brien.

By and large, the lumber crews offered little more than seasonal work. But with the 1903 discovery of silver at Cobalt, Ontario, the Valley's connection to northern Ontario was transformed. The Cobalt silver rush fuelled exploration and development across northern Ontario and northwestern Quebec. The newly born communities of this region absorbed the continual migration of Ottawa Valley families. One of the major centres was the Porcupine region, roughly 900 kilometres north of Toronto.

Unlike the insular, rural culture of the Valley, the mining camps were multi-ethnic and wide open. International travel writer and war correspondent Pierre van Paassen provides this provocative image of the early days of the Porcupine goldfields:

> From South Porcupine, the amusement and relaxation centre of the gold fields, the power and glory had already departed, but…you could still see the prospectors and trappers coming in from the year's search for gold and fox skins. Some of these men, quite a cosmopolitan lot they were, had been to other gold countries, like the Klondike, Mexico or South Africa….They sat on the dilapidated, though once gaudy hotels and saloon bars, rocking their chairs and aiming squirts of tobacco juice at brightly polished brass spittoons.

As the mines became established, the gold rush character was steadily eroded and replaced by the narrow regimen of these company towns. All facets of town life revolved around the rigid production schedules of the gold giants. These mines hired men in the thousands. The gates outside the mines were filled with hungry young men looking for a chance at a steady paycheque. One of those looking to get hired on was a tall, lanky lad from Killaloe, Ontario, named Jack Costello, father of Les Costello.

"The Irish community moved to places like Noranda, Kirkland, Cobalt. It was very tight knit. Once you knew someone was from the Valley you had a friend in whatever town you were in. It was like the same feeling you would have if you were overseas and met someone from Canada."

—*D'Arcy Quinn*

2. A Child Is Born

"Father Costello told us all the time that a funeral wasn't a sad time. 'Whenever someone dies,' he'd say, 'something good will always come out of it.'"

—Shirley McGarry, St. Alphonsus parishioner

"My mother loved the Ottawa Valley stories. She used to tell us about how her brother died. He was in his early 30s and the morning he died the horse broke out of the stable and rushed to his window and just stood there. My mother said things like that didn't happen accidentally. It was a sign."

—Murray Costello, Les Costello's younger brother

The first of the great funerals took place at the Timmins United Church, as a crowd of 1,500 made their way behind the coffins of two Cornish miners. The procession was led by a 100-man choir of fellow "Cousin Jacks" (men from Cornwall, England) singing "Abide with Me." Across town at St. Anthony's Cathedral, the Catholic priests blessed an array of coffins adorned with the Union Jack and Yugoslavian flags.

The next morning, a crowd estimated to be near two thousand people gathered on the steps of the Finnish community hall at the corner of Balsam and Fourth Avenue. A sleigh drew up carrying the coffins of eight Finns and one Ukrainian. The Finnish concert band struck up a lament from the old country and the crowd began trudging along behind. The path in front of the sleighs had been marked out by a layer of evergreen boughs. The bodies were then lowered into a long, sloping trench that had been dug from the frozen ground by hands well used to the unforgiving earth of the Porcupine.

Over a three-day period, 39 men were buried – victims of a horrific underground fire at Hollinger Gold Mine. It was the largest hardrock mining disaster in Canadian history, and the funeral at the Finn Hall was the single largest funeral in the Porcupine history. (The size of this funeral would not be repeated for another 74 years, until the death of Father Les Costello.) In the "ethnic" neighbourhoods of the Porcupine, these mass deaths fuelled rage against the capitalist owners. The result was a number of competing union drives from the anarcho-syndicalists of the One Big Union and the Wobblies (Industrial Workers of the World) through to the Communist-backed Mine Workers Union to the Mine Mill and Smelter Workers Union.

But even in the numbing horror of the great fire, life had to go on. The day after the great funerals, two thousand miners were assembled to return to the depths of the still smoking Hollinger Mine. Meanwhile, over in South Porcupine, the cry of new life was being heard. A baby had come kicking and screaming into this world. His name was Leslie John Thomas Costello. The date was February 16, 1928.

> *"My dad worked at the Dome Mine for 43 years. When he retired, he got a gold watch and a kick in the rear end. I'm not sure he got the gold watch but I know he got a kick in the rear."*
>
> —*Les Costello*

Les was the second child of Jack and Clare (O'Grady) Costello. The other Costello children – Rita (b. 1926), Don (b. 1932), Murray (b. 1934) and Jack (b. 1939) – were tall and fair like their father. Les, however, was small and wiry, with a mop of dark, curly hair. His siblings liked to tease that he had been switched with the baby of an Italian family. Les didn't mind the jibes. After all, he was always the little bugger with the water pistol, the prank or the joke.

There was little to distinguish the Costello family from the multitude of mining and logging families in the Porcupine. Jack Sr. had first come to South Porcupine in 1923 in search of the elusive dream of a steady job. He had been working his way steadily northward through the bush camps and lumber mills since the age of fifteen. When he was a teenager, his father received a small nick in the chest after stepping through the razor wire in the cow field at the family farm in Killaloe one day. He continued on with his field work, giving no thought to the wound. The cut, however, turned septic and within a few days he was dead. Jack was left with the task of trying to support his mother and young siblings.

It was no coincidence that Jack's elusive search for a steady job eventually landed him in the Porcupine. South Porcupine was the gateway to the fabulous Porcupine gold fields. The gold rush had been touched off by the 1909 discovery of the "Golden staircase" – a rich band of gold ore cutting through a mound of quartz outcropping known as the "Big Dome." The Porcupine was now home to three main communities (South Porcupine, Schumacher and Timmins) that had grown up almost overnight to feed three of the largest gold mines in the British Empire – Dome, McIntyre and Hollinger. Numerous smaller gold operations and company townsites dotted the region.

Jack tried his hand at underground gold production at the Dome Mine, but lasted barely a week in the unforgiving depths. The turnover of English-speaking Canadians in the underground gold stopes was 75 per cent in the first month. This hard and dangerous work was the domain of immigrant Slavs and Italians. Jack was reassigned as a carpenter in the mill. In 1925 he returned to the Ottawa Valley to marry Clare O'Grady. He brought her north, as their daughter would later say, "to the end of the world."

Jack Costello is remembered by his children as a "typical Irishman" – laid-back and content with life. Clare, however, was a strong-willed matriarch. She had left the familiarity of a rural Irish farm community for the muddy wooden sidewalks of a frontier town. Wages were low. There was no medical coverage for families. No social assistance. When a breadwinner was injured or killed in the mines, families were left destitute.

In the Valley, the Irish survived the hard times because they stuck together. Clare Costello brought this same protective fierceness to her new neighbours, regardless of whether they spoke the same language or shared the same religion. She knew that the only safety net that existed in this harsh land was the one knitted together by local women.

"Mother was a very giving lady," recalls Rita (Costello) Hogan. "She was always baking for the neighbours, always sewing or knitting for somebody. In those days there was no hospital coverage – babies were born at home. Mother was always bringing soup over to the sick. She didn't work outside the home, but she worked very hard."

As the eldest boy, Les was always very close to his mother. He learned his first lessons in hospitality through the example of Clare Costello. Even at a young age, certain elements that would later be a hallmark of his spirituality were established.

"Thinking about him as a child, he never had much interest in material things," says his sister Rita Hogan. "How he dressed wasn't important to him. Some of what he was to become later was present from a very early age but we never paid any attention to it. We certainly never thought he'd become a priest."

"South Porcupine was a great community to grow up in because the whole community was one. Ethnic backgrounds weren't a factor at all. All the kids growing up knew each other very well. We were all very comfortable in each other's homes, regardless of whether or not their parents could speak any English at all."

—Murray Costello

In the 1930s, South Porcupine was known as a "Finn Town" because of the large Finnish settlement that existed at the edge of town. The local Finnish community hall served as a centre for the whole town. The Finnish community of the Porcupine was divided, as were many of the immigrant neighbourhoods, by the political wars of the old country.

In the Porcupine the dominant Finnish group were "Reds" – supporters of the failed Bolshevik uprising of 1919. They were deeply opposed by fellow countrymen known as the "White Finns" – supporters of the counter-revolution that resulted in a bloody civil war.

In all the mining towns of the Porcupine, the immigrant communities maintained their own ethnic halls – the Polish White Eagle Hall, the Italian Dante Club, the Croatian Hall, the Ukrainian Labour Temple ("Red" Ukrainian), Provista Hall ("White" Ukrainian), Finn Hall ("Red" Finn) and Harmony Hall ("White" Finn).

These halls also served as community centres for a whole array of multi-ethnic children. The Irish Costello children, for example, spent many of their Saturdays watching the concerts and events at the local Finn Hall. Pat Hannigan, who grew up among the Slavic families in neighbouring Schumacher, remembers the Croatian Hall as the centre of life in the town known as "Little Zagreb."

"For the kids, the real centre of the community was the arena," he says. "For teenagers it was the dances at the Croatian Hall."

George Stefanic, a resident of Schumacher, recalls the ethnic dances at the Croatian Hall: "When we were growing up we never had babysitters. As children we went to every event at the Croatian Hall and just slept on the floor while the events took place."

For the Irish, the parish served as a central focus of identity. This is the way it had been since the early days of the Cobalt silver rush, when Father John O'Gorman came up from Eganville to establish the first English-speaking church – St. Patrick's in Cobalt. As the miners moved north, Father O'Gorman moved with them and was instrumental in building Nativity parish in Timmins (known among the locals as the "Irish" church). Throughout the history of the Timmins diocese, Ottawa Valley priests were a dominant presence in the English-speaking churches. The first wave of English-speaking priests in the Timmins diocese was led by Ottawa Valley priests like Father O'Gorman, Father McManus, Father Callaghan, Father Jeffrey and Father McMahon. The second generation of priests was dominated by the presence of priests born to Ottawa Valley families living in the north: Father Costello, Father O'Connor, Father Scully and Father Murray.

The Costellos were active in building St. Joachim's parish in South Porcupine. Clare Costello went to Mass every day. On cold winter mornings when the scheduled altar boys failed to show up for Mass, she hauled Les and his brothers out of bed. Murray Costello learned how to serve the Mass from his older brother.

"I remember the first Mass I served was with Les," he says. "When it came time to change the book after the gospel I went and got the book as instructed while the priest turned his back to me and genuflected in front of the altar. Les told me to go stand at the far end of the altar and wait. I went and stood there with the book and waited. Meanwhile, the priest was standing with his back to me, waiting for me to bring the book. Finally he turned around and said, 'Murray, get over here.' Les thought the whole thing was a helluva joke."

Clare Costello, with her daily Mass attendance, would not be seen in those days as an overly "religious" woman. Catholic families were "outsiders" in the dominant Protestant culture of the day and the community maintained a deep inner discipline based around regular attendance at church. Their faith was deeply imbued with an otherworldly mysticism as evidenced by the Tridentine (Latin) Mass. The priest performed his rituals with his back to the congregation, speaking to God in a language that none of them understood.

Nonetheless, the laity maintained a very rich and tactile faith life centred on weekly devotional exercises – the Rosary, the Friday night novenas and litanies to various saints. Every Catholic family had subscriptions to numerous pious publications dedicated to devotional figures such as the Virgin Mother of Fatima or St. Theresa of Lisieux (the "Little Flower").

Father Des O'Connor, who grew up in the neighbouring gold region of Kirkland Lake, describes a typical Catholic household in those days: "The family rosary was a big priority. You couldn't go out until the rosary was said. If friends came to the door when we were saying the rosary, the Catholics were expected to get on their knees and say the rosary while Protestant friends were expected to sit until it was done."

The rosary is a repetitive call-and-response form of prayer based on a cycle of five "decades" (ten prayers) anchored on the "Hail Mary" prayer. Les Costello maintained a lifelong devotion to this form of prayer.

"Les loved when people could sing or recite poetry. If we [The Flying Fathers] were at a school gymnasium full of school kids or a social in a church hall, he'd go around trying to find out what talents people had. He wanted to celebrate those talents. He'd get the person up to sing a song or recite a poem."

—*D'Arcy Quinn*

Besides the church, the central focus for the Irish families was the kitchen table. It was a world still in the earliest days of radio. The family was the primary source of entertainment – all of it had to be self-made through either story or song. People put great value on a relative who could spin an entertaining yarn or sing a good song. Nothing made the Irish families happier than when they were "getting into the talking."

"Mom loved the stories and the arguments," recalls Murray Costello. "At mealtimes she was right in the middle of it."

The Costellos loved to "mix it up," with Les and his youngest brother, Jack, often competing for theatrics. When Clare was given a bathrobe for Christmas, it set the perfect stage for young Jackie to parade around the house in his mother's new garb.

"We'd sit around the kitchen talking after supper," says Rita. "Les would get up to leave and would stand behind Mom, talking. He'd be tying her apron strings to the chair and then when she got up to say goodbye she'd pull the chair with her." Throughout his adult life, Les loved the gathering of storytellers and singers around a kitchen table.

"Come back to the rectory for a shot of rye." It was an invitation to the friends and storytellers after Sunday Mass in every parish he served. This is how Costello recreated the fun of those after-supper gabfests that had been so much a part of that little family home on Commercial Avenue in South Porcupine.

3. The Game

"I remember being very young and wanting to emulate Les. One night, after a Friday night hockey game, he and a friend decided to skate across the lake and they wouldn't let me come. Once they had taken off I followed them, staying just far enough behind so that I could see them. It was one of those northern nights – clear with the black ice. Every stride you took, the ice buckled in front of you so you chased the cracks as you skated.

Finally, when they got to the other side, Les saw me and he really gave me shit. He said, 'You don't ever skate alone on the ice. You always have a partner because so many things could go wrong.' I got it from him and then I got it from my old man when I got home."

—*Murray Costello*

Life was the game. Not a game of refs, coaches and overprotective hockey parents. Not a game of timed shifts and trained drills. This wasn't the kitschy Canadiana archetype of a dad, his son and a Saturday morning rink that is now trotted out every winter for donut, hamburger and hardware chain advertising.

This was a game of children. It had no real beginning or end. It was fluid, formless and open to as many kids who showed up with their makeshift goalie pads and taped-together sticks. The game started when the ice froze in November and carried on until the final slushy thaw in May.

"It was the game that brought all the kids together, from Connaught Hill out to the highway," recalls Murray Costello. "There was no TV. When things got too ruckus in the home, they'd order us outside. 'Get your coat on. Get outside.' We had to do something because if we just stood there we'd freeze. So we played road hockey and the games went on and on and on. It was wonderful. We never wanted to come back in no matter what the temperature."

Rita Hogan remembers her brothers always being involved in the games of the season.

"Sports was the centre of life for the boys. They were always playing hockey or baseball. They played road hockey all the time. They used Eaton's catalogues for shin pads and frozen horse turds for pucks."

The game was played outdoors – either on a shovelled-out spot on the local lake or on one of the many open-air rinks that were set up with proper boards (and occasionally night lighting). In the mining camps across northern Ontario, this never-ending game served as a virtual assembly line of future hockey greats.

Murray Costello, who is the former president of the Canadian Hockey Association and board member of the International Ice Hockey Federation, believes that modern children's hockey has lost some of the creative freedom of the pre-war game.

"We benefited from the fact that, at the time we were growing up, the game was still unregimented. It hadn't moved indoors with the 50-minute hour, with 10 minutes for the Zamboni. We played on the lake every day. Every weekend we were down there skating and chasing people. Maybe we were the last generation to grow up like that."

It was a game that was perfectly suited to the restless energy of Les Costello.

"Les was a fast skater," recalls Pete Babando, a former neighbour and NHL star. "He was a rugged hockey player. You could say dirty but it was a give-and-take game. He didn't back down, that's for sure."

At the local Golden Avenue Public School, Les Costello was seen by some as a natural leader, by others as a natural ringleader.

"He was a hyper kid with boundless energy," says Murray Costello. "He never sat still. He was bouncing, moving. Any challenge that came up, he was up for. Without sports he would have driven everybody nuts."

What saved Les from being tagged a troublemaker was the fact that he took to academia with the same ease as he took to the ice. His high marks surprised some who noticed that Les just didn't seem to spend much time on homework. As Murray Costello says, Les was blessed with an "outstanding memory."

"He could read things and digest them and then spew them back at you. School was never difficult for him. He loved to read."

Costello's love of reading and word play drew him into the world of poetry. He kept a little black scribbler that he filled with poems about friends, neighbours and local characters, such as Ozzie Bowes, who ran the local rink. The poems were in the simple rhyming styles of Robert Service or Henri Drummond.

When he was fourteen, Les Costello wrote an eleven-stanza poem to his sports hero, New York Yankee baseball player Lou Gehrig.

In the Hall of Fame there lies a name
A hero of modern ball
He faced his fate with a manly gait
Lou Gehrig inscribed on the wall.

The retirement speech Gehrig gave at Yankee Stadium on July 4, 1939, was shown in countless newsreels around the world. We see Gehrig, a man with a fabled baseball career, poised at the edge of the looming abyss of a painful and early death from amyotrophic lateral sclerosis (ALS, which was named Lou Gehrig's disease after his diagnosis). Les Costello, like countless other youth around North America, was deeply influenced by Gehrig's dignity in the face of such dismal prospects.

The memorial game full of sadness and fame
Would fill the best man's eyes with tears.
And the talk Lou gave before entering the grave
Will be one remembered for years.

Within two months of Gehrig's speech, the world was plunged into war. In Lou Gehrig, the adolescent Costello found a symbol through which to see the world amidst the darkness of the Nazi war.

And now listen to me, on land, or on the sea
Let's face death with courage so brave
And we'll beat the Huns with our ships and our guns
An example of Lou Gehrig from his grave.

Looking at this poem in an age of multi-millionaire sports stars, it is difficult not to be cynical about ball players being treated as heroes. But throughout his life, Les Costello liked to recite his poem about Lou Gehrig, often attributing the work to "Anonymous." Clearly, Les never gave up on his early belief that the athlete, like the priest, was called to represent a higher ideal.

"In the 1930s, hockey players from all over were coming into the Porcupine looking for work. If you could skate, you could get a job. They had very good teams here – hockey, baseball, soccer."

—Pete Babando, former NHL player

"I remember vividly my dad coming home from work in the winter and asking my mother what the day had been like. He left home in the dark and came home in the dark so he never saw the sun."

—Pat Hannigan

For adults, life in the Porcupine was anything but a game. The Great Depression of the 1930s had devastated the economy of Canada. The burgeoning gold mines of the north became a magnet for thousands of unemployed men. These men gathered in shanty camps at the edge of town and waited every morning outside the gates of the mines in the hope of being hired. Backlashes against immigrant workers resulted in numerous "ethnic" riots in the various mining towns. For those lucky enough to get hired, the mines maintained rigid production schedules with men working six or even seven days a week.

Bob Miner, a neighbour of the Costello family, gave this account of the working conditions of Porcupine mines in an interview in 1976:

It was rough work. You were completely at the mercy of the company. They cared less for a man than they did a shovel because a shovel cost money while a man could be replaced merely by going to the gate and picking out a strong one. At some mines, men were manhandled by the superintendents like cattle – their muscles being felt before they were hired.

Among those streaming into the northern mining camps were top-notch hockey players from across the country. They were looking for the chance for a steady income on the payroll of a company team. In each of the mining camps, the mine owners maintained semi-pro baseball, soccer and hockey teams as entertainment for the largely single, and otherwise potentially troublesome, male workforce.

Former Toronto Maple Leaf Gus Mortson remembers the Depression-era teams: "During the 1930s the mines used to promote hockey considerably. We had players in Kirkland Lake like Bill Durnan and Johnny Crawford. There was a whole bunch playing who could have held their own as pros. Watching them was a big incentive for kids."

It has become part of the Canadian myth that generations of youth built their dreams around the dynasties of the "Original Six," but the history of the NHL is anything but a straight lineage. The Toronto Maple Leafs, for example, didn't even exist for the first decade of the National Hockey League. Until the 1930s, the league was made up of such teams as the Pittsburgh Pirates, the Montreal Maroons and the New York Americans. With radio still in its infancy, rural fans were likely to pay more attention to the fortunes of regional hockey leagues than the NHL.

In the north, young hockey dreamers pinned their hopes on a chance to play for one of the gold mines. Pete Babando, who later signed to the NHL, remembers that his original hockey aspirations hadn't extended any further than the local mining league. Pat Hannigan, who was one of three Hannigan brothers to make it to the pros, recalls that the opportunity to head south simply wasn't available in the pre-war years.

"My oldest brother never made it past the Hollinger [Mine] Greenshirts. He never thought of being able to go away to play hockey."

J.P. Bickell, top dog of McIntyre-Porcupine Mines Ltd., personified the connection between the gold-mining economy and hockey. In 1927, Bickell sold his interest in Toronto's pro hockey team (the St. Patrick's) to a young upstart named Conn Smythe. The team was renamed the Maple Leafs.

In 1930, Smythe returned to Bickell looking for cash to build an audacious new hockey "palace." The Depression was at its height and Toronto financial circles were starved of investment dollars. But the gold mines were booming. Bickell ponied up the cash and, in exchange, was brought back into Toronto's hockey world as the newly named President of the Toronto Maple Leafs. A year later, Maple Leaf Gardens was officially opened.

In 1938, Bickell set out to build a smaller, but no less impressive, arena in the shadow of the McIntyre Gold Mine. The McIntyre Arena was the finest community centre/hockey arena anywhere in the north. The building featured a hockey rink with the same colour pattern of seats as the Gardens. In addition to an indoor rink, the building boasted a curling rink, a mirrored skating rink for female figure skaters, a bowling alley, auditorium, coffee shop and gymnasium. The gym was run by ex-boxer Johnny Bagordo. Youth were allowed in any time of the day or night to work on the heavy bag and weights.

On the ice rink of "the Mac," local hockey boys got their first taste of what the big time felt like. "We used to have the playoffs for our school teams at the McIntyre arena," recalls Pat Hannigan. "Up until then, the only games we'd ever played were outside. We had always relied on a sleigh, a butter box and two hockey stick handles pushing our equipment to the rink and putting on our skates and gear when they were already frozen. At the arena there were showers and proper dressing rooms."

Gregory Reynolds describes the intensity of the interschool showdowns held at the Mac: "When the playoffs occurred there was always a lot of fighting in the stands [between the Catholic and public school teams], sparked equally by religious beliefs and the need to attract young girls. Each year it got worse, until eventually the school boards decided the racial and religious disharmony wasn't worth the benefits of having a school champion."

Racial disharmony, however, was part and parcel of the hiring policies of both the mines and the NHL. Jobs at the mines were divided up along an internal hierarchy of ethnic and religious gradations. Until the 1960s, it was almost unheard of for an ethnic worker or a Roman Catholic to be hired to a supervisory job at any of the northern mines. In the early 1940s, McIntyre Mine hired three young hotshots sight unseen – only to fire them as soon as they arrived in Timmins. McIntyre's management balked at finding out that their new line of aces was black. The "Coloured Line" of Manny McIntyre, Herbie and Ossie Carnegie had been barred by the NHL thanks to Conn Smythe's (and Bickell's) refusal to allow blacks to play professionally.

The "Coloured Line" was dumped by Bickell's local team but was immediately picked up by a small local gold operation, the Buffalo Ankerite Mine. The "Coloured Line" would have been a top line in the pro hockey leagues had the NHL been willing to break the colour barrier. The multi-ethnic fans of the Porcupine didn't seem to share the racial disdain of their bosses. The Coloured Line became a favourite of local fans.

"I watched the Coloured Line play in the Miners' League," recalls Pat Hannigan. "They were the best line to ever play in the Miners' League. They were immensely popular in the north because there wasn't the prejudice as there was in the cities. They could play hockey and that was all that people cared about."

The "Coloured Line" was a vivid example of the exciting brand of regional hockey that set a high standard for young hockey players like Les Costello.

4. A Church on Skates

"At sixteen I had all these offers to go away to play hockey. I could have gone to Galt, Guelph, Barrie or St. Mike's. I went to Les and asked him what I should do.

'I don't want to tell you,' he said, 'because if it doesn't work for you, you'll have me to blame for the rest of your life.'

I said, 'I'm not looking for you to make a decision. I just want to be able to get the benefit of your experience because you've been there ahead of me.'

'I'll only tell you one thing,' he said. 'I went to St. Mike's because people told me I would make friendships there that will last me the rest of my life. Now that I've been there, I think that's true.'

This was good enough for me. I went to St. Mike's and in my view Les was right."

– Murray Costello

When Father Henry Carr organized the first hockey team at St. Michael's College School in Toronto in 1907, he wasn't simply looking to give the boys a chance to skate off some steam. Carr wanted a team of winners. These winners would be entrusted with the task of taking Catholic pride, scholasticism and athletics out of the religious ghetto and into the mainstream.

The Basilian fathers had been running St. Michael's College for nearly 50 years. But the social and political structure of the city, like the province at that time, was firmly anti-Catholic. Orange Toronto was known as "Little Belfast." The annual Orange Day parade in Toronto often took over five hours to complete, with numbers in the 1920s being above 10,000 participants a year. (It wasn't until 1972 that a city leader, Mayor David Crombie, dared snub the Orangemen's parade.)

Carr wanted his fledgling "Irish Machine" to bump sticks against the best Protestant schools. In doing so, St. Mike's would establish a public Catholic presence that was otherwise out of reach in a city dominated by the old Family Compact and Mason rings.

In their very first year, St. Mike's took the Toronto Prep League title from the more powerful Protestant schools. With the success of this school league, Carr began putting together a squad of talented over-age players to compete for the Senior Ontario Hockey Association (OHA) title. In 1910, the St. Michael's Majors won the coveted Allan Cup. The success of St. Mike's helped build a strong base of hockey support in Toronto that professional hockey would later capitalize on.

Carr adopted hockey the way countless missionaries during the Dark Ages usurped the existing pagan traditions of northern Europe. Much of the colourful and esoteric elements in the cult of the saints can be attributed to the blending of local pagan traditions with the then-rising Catholic hegemony. Historian Christopher Dawson described this cultural appropriation in his book *Religion and the Rise of Western Culture.*

> In this twilight world, it was inevitable that the Christian ascetic and saint should acquire some of the features of the pagan shaman and demi-god; that his prestige should depend upon his power as a wonder-worker and that men should seek his decision in the same way as they had formerly resorted to the shrine of the pagan oracle.

Just as the mission Church in the Dark Ages baptized the animistic practices of the Gauls, the Catholic Church in Canada baptized the wrist shot and the body check. And they succeeded. The game was championed in Catholic schools. Priests and nuns acted as coaches, managers and supporters of local Catholic teams.

In the Timmins diocese, the hockey/Church connection was well established from its earliest days. Father Martindale ran boys' teams in Cobalt. Father Caulfield ran the St. Patrick's Shamrocks out of Nativity parish in Timmins. Holy Name parish in Kirkland Lake, which features two embossed figures on its church columns – saintly-looking hockey players in front of an imposing crucifix – was home to a powerful junior hockey team known as the Holy Name Irish.

But St. Mike's remained the beacon for this blending of athletics and piety. The Basilians looked to hockey to create a breed of tough, outgoing and spiritual young men as a base for the Canadian priesthood. Les Costello would be one of their success stories.

> *"In the 1940s, there were fourteen outdoor rinks in the Town of Timmins, [including] one at each one of the public and separate schools.... Each nationality had its own school – Moneta [Public] for the Italians; Holy Family for the Irish, Ukrainians and Polish; Jacques Cartier for the French; Birch Street and Central School for the English Protestants. A boy from one school didn't go to another school's rink unless he was accompanied by half a dozen friends."*
>
> —*Gregory Reynolds, The Rinkmen*

By age fifteen, Les Costello had established a local reputation as a tough player. He wasn't exactly a graceful skater, but he had a helluva stride. His presence on the ice was more like that of a ricocheting cue ball on a snooker table – continually scattering plays and formations. At 5' 8" and 160 lbs, Costello was relatively small, but he left enough gouges in opposing players for them to stay clear of him whenever possible.

In the Porcupine, local youth hockey existed at three levels – unorganized play on the outdoor rinks; organized grade school leagues; and, for those who could make the cut, junior hockey. The local junior team was the Holman Pluggers (named after a local mining machine company). In a community awash with hockey-crazed youth, the Holman Pluggers had the pick of the best. Local boys Allan Stanley, Pete Babando and "Doc" Prentice were on the line. Bill Barilko was a stick boy for the team, jumping at the chance to fill in as a goalie when the team was short-handed at practice. (Bill Barilko would later score the most famous goal in the history of the Gardens – the 1951 overtime goal against Montreal. For years his No. 5 sweater was only one of two Leaf numbers officially retired by the franchise; the other was Ace Bailey.) In the fall of 1942, Costello was invited to join this elite local squad. Jack Sr., however, was having none of it. He had no intention of letting his son spend his nights firing pucks at the Mac when he should be hitting the books.

Les maintained high marks in school, and in the fall of 1943, Jack relented and let him try out for the Pluggers. At age sixteen Les Costello had finally graduated from the ice pond. He was now a forward with the Pluggers. Les signed on to a team of champions.

With Les on the front lines, the Holman Pluggers fought their way to the Ontario championships. They faced off against St. Catharines, a team that had dominated the league throughout the war years. But the Pluggers, for the second time in two years, came home with the bragging rights for all of Ontario. Les's outstanding presence on the team had drawn the attention of the priests at St. Mike's. They invited him to Toronto to complete his education. It was an invitation into the exclusive world of the Toronto Maple Leafs.

Les went to St. Mike's in the fall of 1944 for Grade 11. Looking to avoid an emotional farewell on the station platform, he said goodbye to his mother and siblings at the door of their Commercial Avenue home. Twenty-one years earlier, his father had come north on the train, looking to settle down. Now Les was leaving, carrying with him his gear bag, his stick, his skates and dreams of a much bigger world. The importance of Les Costello's trip to St. Mike's was not lost on younger hockey players around town.

"The dream of going away to play started with players like Les Costello," explains Pat Hannigan. "All of a sudden we saw guys like Cossie and my brothers [Ray and Gordie] getting to play at St. Mike's and then they were making it onto the Leafs. This really encouraged us younger guys to play and work hard."

Over the years, a veritable Who's Who of hockey stars went through the St. Mike's organization, including Tim Horton, Dave Keon, Frank Mahovlich, Gerry Cheevers, Ted Lindsay and Eric Lindros. Father Carr had dreamed that these young heroes would represent the best interests of Catholic identity. By the 1940s, however, the school's hockey program was under the control of the caesar of Carlton Street – Conn Smythe.

St. Mike's was an integral part of the Toronto Maple Leafs organization. Smythe maintained two junior teams – St. Mike's and the Toronto Marlboros ("Marlies"). Officially, St. Mike's was the team for Leaf prospects who were still in school, while the Marlies was reserved for those outside of school. But the real distinction was religious – St. Mike's was Smythe's Catholic team while the Marlies was Smythe's Protestant team. The division of the fan base also fell along religious lines.

"St. Mike's sold its soul to Conn Smythe," says Pat Hannigan. "They wanted to be the Notre Dame of Canada. They did whatever Conn Smythe wanted. If a Protestant couldn't make the [Toronto] Marlies, they'd get bumped onto St. Mike's and the school would take them."

Smythe never let the young St. Mike's players forget who was calling the shots. Murray Costello, who was signed to Chicago on his sixteenth birthday, tells this story about Smythe's influence on the team:

"St. Mike's let me in because my brother had been there and they thought I could contribute to the team. Every time we went into the Gardens to practise, all the Leaf chattel were able to walk through to the dressing rooms, but because I wasn't Leaf property, I would always be stopped and have to show my pass. Smythe wanted it that way."

When the Leafs spotted a hot young prospect such as Johnny McCormack from Edmonton or Frank Mahovlich from Schumacher,

Smythe had them shipped to St. Mike's. Other youth worked hard to get the priests at the school to let them attend because it was a way of getting noticed by the Leaf scouts. Gus Mortson, a young Protestant kid from Kirkland Lake, was accepted at the school along with his buddy Ted Lindsay on the urging of a local priest who thought the two would add muscle to the Irish Machine.

"St. Mike's was a good school," recalls Gus Mortson. "We were treated like kings there. After school we'd go down to the Gardens to practise for games."

It was during one of these practices that Mortson was scouted by the Leafs and signed to a coveted A form. (The league had three levels of signing rights, known as A, B and C forms. Each team was allowed to sign four players to the exclusivity of an A form.)

The eager young men who headed down for the annual St. Mike's Easter tryouts saw the school as a ticket to a better world. Pat Hannigan was part of a group of Schumacher boys who were invited down one year.

"We decided that, being from Schumacher and wanting to make the team, we were going to kick the shit out of everybody at the tryout," he remembers.

The boys took to the ice for an opening scrimmage. Immediately, the Schumacher lads went to work – cross checking, hitting, slamming other boys into the glass. The play degenerated so quickly that the whistle was blown and the scrimmage called off. The result of this carnage? Both Pat Hannigan and his buddy Peter Buchman were immediately invited into the St. Mike's family.

Says Hannigan, "They thought that the guys from the north were the absolute toughest goddamned things they'd ever seen in their lives. And we were, because we didn't want to go back to work in the mines. We needed to get out of the north and the only way to do it was with our skates."

On the ice, Les established a reputation as a tough northern scrapper. Off the ice, his outgoing personality drew friends easily. Johnny

McCormack remembers him as a "real shit disturber." And yet, Les carried with him a deep piety that was often not recognized by other students. He attended Mass regularly and was often found in the chapel praying the Stations of the Cross that hung along the chapel walls.

Costello's competitiveness and piety embodied the main goals pursued by the Basilian fathers. But these two goals were not natural bedfellows and resulted in an underlying tension in the school culture. While some priests treated the young hotshots as heroes, others saw them as jocks dragging down the higher goals of Catholic education.

"Some priests," says Hannigan, "simply refused to teach us. When we'd come into class they'd say, 'You're a hockey player. Sit at the back and don't bother putting up your hand to answer any questions.'"

Some former St. Mike's students say the school culture was unfairly weighted in favour of the star players. Murray Costello disagrees. He says that despite being treated as hockey heroes, there was no free ride for the star athletes.

"In my view, the school went out of its way to make sure you didn't get a swelled head. St. Mike's wasn't an easy ride. It was a rough schedule. If you got home from a game in Barrie at two o'clock in the morning, they expected you to be up for school in the morning."

In the spring of 1945, Costello's team went up against the Moose Jaw Canucks in a best-of-seven showdown for the Memorial Cup. It was a national event.

Joe Primeau, a St. Mike's alumnus and famed hero of the Leaf's Kid Line (Primeau, Charlie Conacher and Busher Jackson, which rocked the 1931–32 Stanley Cup playoffs), ruled the bench for the Irish Machine. St. Mike's came out flying, taking the opener 8-3. Costello counted for a goal. Moose Jaw came back for the second game, winning 5-3 in front of nearly 13,000 fans.

St. Mike's took the third game with Costello pocketing the winning goal midway through the third period. Over 14,000 fans jammed into the Gardens to watch Costello cut down the westerners.

"They played the Memorial Cup on a Saturday afternoon," recalls Murray Costello. "The lineup for tickets was right around the block of Maple Leaf Gardens. There was so much excitement for those games. It was a very exciting time."

The city was buzzing with Memorial Cup fever even though the night games at the Gardens involved the Maple Leafs fighting for the coveted Stanley Cup. St. Mike's took game four and then shut it all down in game five for the first Memorial Cup win for St. Mike's in ten years. Paid attendance for the series was 65,437.

Costello's imprint was all over the victory. Timmins sportswriter Doug McLellan later described the line of Costello, Sloan and MacKell as "a line that is generally considered one of the all-time greats in junior hockey."

In 1946, St. Mike's lost in the seventh game of the finals to Winnipeg. It was still an exciting nail-biter. The following year, Costello and St. Mike's were back for another go at the Moose Jaw Canucks, only this time, Toronto's boys were playing in the western cities of Winnipeg, Regina and Moose Jaw.

Described in the press as the "smoothest team to come out of the east in years," St. Mike's, led by the line of Ed Sandford, Les Costello and Fleming MacKell, "passed the disc around like a hot biscuit to collect a baker's dozen in the scoring points."

Costello scored a hat trick in this 12-3 victory, and his linemates did their share, too: Sanford counted for five goals and MacKell for two.

The second game was rough but still no contest. It was fought with fists and sticks and resulted in a 6-1 victory by the polished Toronto team. At this first national final ever played in Moose Jaw, Les Costello bagged another goal.

By game three, the western fans were turning hostile. After St. Mike's moved up 8-1 (including another goal by Costello), the Winnipeg game had to be stopped. Angry fans were pelting the ice with bottles.

Four times, play was stopped and the rink cleared of broken glass. Four times, the bottle-throwing started up again to force St. Mike's off the ice. The next day, the local Regina paper issued an editorial entitled "We Hang Our Heads in Shame." The editors described the game as "worse than the Stanley Cup riot in Chicago in 1944. It was definitely more vicious."

By the time game number four rolled around a few nights later, the western crowds were as dispersed and dispirited as the Moose Jaw players. Costello's team took an easy win for the second Memorial Cup in three years.

Murray Costello puts the St. Mike's team of those years in perspective.

"Les played on one of the best junior teams that ever existed. His energy and skating abilities allowed him to meld in with that team very easily. He was a key guy for them and played very well."

Just how powerful this team was is clear from the number of team members that made the jump to pro hockey. Gus Mortson, of the 1945 team, was already playing for the Maple Leafs. Joining him in the NHL were St. Mike's players Red Kelly, Flem MacKell, Jimmy Thompson, Ray Hannigan, Johnny McCormack, Tod Sloan and Les Costello.

Even more striking is the fact that, out of this junior hockey "Dream Team," a total of five players made the choice to enter the seminary. Dave Bauer, one of St. Mike's best young prospects, joined the Basilians instead of going to the NHL. (Father Bauer later formed Canada's first national hockey team. In 1961 he coached St. Mike's to the only Memorial Cup to be won by the school since the 1947 victory. Following this win, Father Bauer put an end to Henry Carr's dream by disbanding the St. Mike's Majors. Bauer felt that the pursuit of hockey was no longer compatible with the educational goals of the school.) Bauer was joined in the priesthood by Ted McLean. Johnny McCormack played one year of hockey in Tulsa, then went into the seminary – only to drop out and go back to hockey. Ray Hannigan stayed with hockey but embraced a late calling to the priesthood. So when Les Costello made the decision to join the priesthood, he wasn't exactly breaking new ground.

Johnny McCormack attributes this strikingly high number of seminary applicants to the influence of the priests at St. Mike's. "It was a fabulous school and the priests had a big influence on us."

It would be almost unheard of today to imagine the top-notch junior hockey team in the country as a potential breeding ground for priests. Pat Hannigan, however, says it was a sign of the times.

"In those days, these young guys were quite religious. They didn't know beans about the Bible, but their mothers brought them up to be very respectful of the Church."

Costello would later tell the media that the seeds of the priesthood were firmly planted by the priests at St. Mike's. In the culture of this school of champions, two strong undercurrents were running – either to the NHL or to the seminary door.

5. Lord Stanley's Ring

"In those days, when you got signed to the NHL there was the owner, the manager and a lawyer and you were by yourself. They threw a contract at you. If you didn't want to sign it you could head back home."

—Pete Babando

"All the Irish Catholics played in Pittsburgh [the farm team] and all the Protestants played in Toronto. There were many Protestant players who made the Leafs who weren't as good as the Catholics playing in Pittsburgh."

—Pat Hannigan

The rookie. Of the hundreds of potential golden youth who come forward for the annual draft, one always stands apart. Some, like Bobby Orr and Wayne Gretzky, seem to have been prepared for this moment since childhood. The value of this rookie is marked in the salary he commands through a crafty agent. If he meets or surpasses the hype, he will become a symbol of everything that is great about "us" and "our" game. If he stumbles, he will become a sacrificial symbol of the excess and greed that we have come to hate in hockey.

It wasn't always this way. In the post-war years, the rookie was simply a lunch-pail junior struggling to find a spot in a hostile closed shop. The NHL employed only 120 players, while a thousand equally good replacements toiled in the minor leagues across Canada and the United States.

"In those days you used to have to play six years in the minors to develop your skills before you ever got called up," says Pat Hannigan. "It was very hard to break into the NHL. If one or two new players came up in a season it was a big deal. There were tons of great hockey players and most of them never made the National Hockey League."

Conn Smythe had a lock on the best players coming out of English Canada. He also had a lock on the pay these players would receive. The six teams kept seven basic "lists" for maintaining control over the available stock of players. Potential players were signed to either the A, B, C tryout forms, the Voluntarily Retired list, the Sponsorship List, the Inactive list, the Players Reserve list or the Negotiation List. If a team discovered a teen outside their organization (from junior hockey or farm teams), it could simply "sign" the youth to the Negotiation List – with or without the youth's agreement. This would give them all rights to the player.

Once players were identified as potential pro material they were signed to the standard C form. Players as young as sixteen were signed to the C form by one of the six teams. The form provided the player with $125 for signing, along with the promise of a further $1,000 after he turned pro. Once signed, the player lost all rights to negotiate for a better offer.

Pat Hannigan refused to sign the C form. He had already seen two other brothers put under the thumb of Conn Smythe. His older brother, Gord (Hopalong) Hannigan, had to quit professional hockey and get a regular job because he wasn't earning enough money to feed his family. The other brother, Ray, had been rookie of the year in the American League and was still unable to win an invite to the Leafs training camp.

"Smythe was a prick of epic proportions," says Pat Hannigan.

Needless to say, when Pat's turn came to make his way into Maple Leaf Gardens, he was well aware of the dictatorial style of Conn Smythe.

"When I turned pro I wouldn't sign the C form. I wanted $2,500 to go pro. Conn Smythe flew my dad down from the mines and said, 'Take your boy into that office and see if he has any brains.' But my dad didn't want me to sign, either. He wanted me to come home and go back to school. He'd already lost two boys to hockey."

Hannigan's hardball tactics eventually resulted in a $2,500 signing fee, but it came at a high price. Smythe shipped him off to a series of teams in the minor leagues.

"I had been the leading scorer in the first ten games of Leaf training camp when they took me aside and said, 'You're going down to Rochester.' I was walking out of the hotel with my suitcase when George Armstrong asked me where I was going. I told him I was being sent down to Rochester. He just shook his head."

Gus Mortson was called up to the Leafs for the 1946–47 season. He was offered $4,000 to play 50 games ($80 a game). After signing, the owners added ten more dates to the schedule. Smythe called Mortson back and offered him $50 a game for the extra ten games. There was no haggling.

"The one thing about Smythe was that he never reneged on what he promised," says Mortson. "But he sure was cheap."

Commercial endorsements did little to improve the financial fortunes of star players. Mortson, a crowd favourite, was chosen to take part in an advertising campaign to endorse Beehive Corn Syrup. His pay consisted of four free quarts of corn syrup.

When Les Costello turned pro in the fall of 1947, it was a given that he would be shipped off to the Leaf farm team in Pittsburgh. He joined his St. Mike's teammates Flem Mackell and Tod Sloan on the line with the Pittsburgh Hornets. His presence was immediately felt. In 68 games with the Hornets, Costello racked up 32 goals and counted for 22 assists. His aggressive style was noticed.

"Les showed no mercy," recalls Pat Hannigan. "You think Gordie Howe was Mr. Elbows? No, Costello was Mr. Elbows. He was a shit disturber on the ice."

This gladiatorial approach was exactly what the NHL expected from its hungry young players. After one particularly bloody free-for-all at the Gardens, Conn Smythe expressed his mock horror to sportswriter Scott Young: "If we don't stamp out this kind of stuff we're going to have to print more tickets."

Up in the majors that year, the Leafs were pushing towards their third consecutive Cup. Coach Hap Day had put together a lineup that would stand as one of the greatest Leaf dynasties ever – Ted "Teeder" Kennedy, Turk Broda, Syl Apps, Max Bentley, Gus Mortson and "Bashing" Bill Barilko. Looking to solidify this team in the semi-finals against Boston, Hap Day decided to bring up Les Costello. Gus Mortson says that even on this super team, Costello was a force to be reckoned with.

"Les was such a good player. The first time he came on the ice with the Leafs he scored a goal."

"It was a huge event when Les got called up to the Leafs," says Murray Costello. "They beat Boston 4-2 and he scored one or two goals. I remember hearing Foster Hewitt on the radio saying, 'Costello shoots, he scores!' It just grabbed me. I told my mom, 'Someday you're going to hear that again.'"

In game three, the Beantown fans jumped the ice and went after the Leaf players. The riot demonstrated the nasty style that typified the series. The Leafs, however, took the semis in five and then knocked off Detroit for the coveted Cup.

The book *Images of Glory: A Photographic History of the Leafs* contains a photograph of Les Costello following the victory over Boston. He is standing with his arm around fellow players Vic Lynn and Teeder Kennedy. In the centre of the picture is coach Hap Day.

Pat Hannigan points out that Costello's Stanley Cup ring – received in his first year of pro play – was a feat not to be underestimated.

"He almost forced his way onto the Leafs because he was so bloody good and so tough. They couldn't ignore him. He was on a team that won the Cup and it happened so early in his career."

The Cup is the source of such mystique among hockey players that it's considered bad luck for a player who has not won the finals even to touch the silver idol. Such subservience was lost on Les Costello. When it came time to put his name on the Cup, he deliberately supplied the wrong name, telling the engraver his name was Lester.

"Why would you do such a thing?" his mother asked him when she found out.

"Oh well," he shrugged, "it sounded good at the time."

Costello later sold his coveted Stanley Cup ring to help a poor family in his parish.

The 1948–49 season began with a home-opener loss to Boston. Les scored the only Leaf goal during his first shift on the ice. He played a further fifteen games with the Leafs before being rotated back down to Pittsburgh. Such a move was typical treatment of young players. The Leafs just didn't keep very many open slots for wingers. Costello played 46 games in Pittsburgh that season, with 13 goals and 31 assists. The Leafs ended the season with another Stanley Cup ring.

In 1949–50, Les played 70 games in Pittsburgh and was brought up for one game in the playoffs. The Leaf dynasty faltered this year, with Boston taking the Cup back to Beantown. The winning goal was scored eight minutes into double overtime of the seventh game by Les Costello's childhood neighbour Pete Babando.

Costello was a potentially great player but he lacked the "discipline" for Smythe's organization. Costello's free-wheeling spirit didn't fit well with Smythe's top-down organization. Players were expected to play and live the way the coach and Smythe dictated. Father M.J. Scully, who came to know Les at the seminary, says Costello was bounced down to Pittsburgh because his rebel attitude ran afoul of Smythe.

"Les treated everybody the same. He didn't defer to anybody. He tangled with Conn Smythe and got shipped down to Pittsburgh. Connie didn't like this brash young player from South Porcupine."

Costello wasn't the only one to chafe at the short leash of Carlton Street's head office. When Johnny "the Goose" McCormack got married at the beginning of the 1951 season, he was given an immediate ticket out of Toronto.

"We pay you to play, not to get married," said Smythe, shipping him down to Pittsburgh.

Perhaps the most telling story about Costello's time with the Leafs comes from team captain Teeder Kennedy. After one loss, Costello came into the dressing room whistling casually, as if he didn't have a care in the world.

Kennedy went up to Costello right away. "Hey, rook, you don't go around whistling after a loss, do you understand me?"

Hannigan says that whistling after a loss would leave you as "dead meat" in the Leaf organization of the time.

Not being able to whistle in the shower may have seemed like a small issue, but it left an impression on Les Costello. He loved hockey because it combined his passions for speed and freedom. Winning and losing was a secondary concern. This is the game he learned on the open ponds of the Porcupine. Neither Hap Day nor Smythe was going to change Costello's views.

Murray Costello explains, "The game was a joy for him to play. It was exhilaration to play, but the rest of it – the adulation, the money, even the Stanley Cup, didn't mean anything to him."

6. The Summer of '50

"One time, I mentioned to Father Les that I saw his picture at Maple Leaf Gardens when he was with the Leafs. I told him, 'Oh, you must have had all the girls after you.' Father Les just responded, 'Nah, nah, nah. You just want me to tell you about my past. No way.' He just wouldn't tell you anything about his past."

—*Margo (Quinn) Young*

Les Costello came home in the summer of 1950 driving a brand-new Mercury. The fancy car was *de rigueur* for a member of a Stanley Cup–winning team. For a 22-year-old boy from the Porcupine, he was living the Canadian dream. While other young men his age were taking the daily cage ride into the depths of the gold fields, Costello had come home a star. But even behind the wheel of a glamorous car, his lack of interest in the trappings of league success was obvious.

"He didn't drive that new car well," recalls Murray Costello. "He didn't take care of it. All he did was play ball all summer."

Les spent the summer anchored in left field of the Hollinger Park. He was a regular with the Porcupine Combines, one of three local teams (along with the Hollinger Gold Miners and the McIntyre Mac Men) competing in a northern senior ball league. (Other teams included Kirkland Lake, Iroquois Falls and a team of U.S. servicemen from the radar base at Ramore, Ontario.) The ball games were played at either the McIntyre Mine ball field or under the imposing shadow of the

Hollinger Mine No. 26 shaft. Hundreds of fans regularly filed into the bleachers at the park to watch the Sunday afternoon games.

Les was a crowd favourite. Summer ball provided a freedom that wasn't available in the pro leagues. For Les, having a crowd laugh with him, or at him, was as good as any home run. He wasn't simply a damned good ball player, he was an entertainer. These were skills he would later employ on the Flying Fathers.

Accounts of his ball-playing antics are still told today.

There was the time that Ray Hannigan hit a line drive in a game between the Combines and the Mac Men. The ball came whizzing into far left field. Les was moving backwards, intent on a pop fly – until his progress was stopped by a snow fence. Ever the showman, he dived over the fence only to realize he had miscalculated. The ball was going to fall short of the fence.

It was one thing to dive over the fence when it had been bent in the direction Costello wanted to go, but getting back over was a whole different matter. The crowd roared with laughter as Costello struggled with the wobbly fence. When the ball hit the ground just beyond his reach he was forced to run the length around the fence. The result? An inside-the-park home run and howls of appreciation from the fans.

Another time, Les was standing on third base razzing the fans and the opposing Hollinger team. While Costello monkeyed about, Hollinger third baseman Frank Chase walked over to confer with the Hollinger pitcher. Costello failed to notice that the pitcher had slipped Chase the ball. Chase returned to his post and as Costello stepped off the bag, Chase tagged him out. Costello's cursing could be heard even above the roaring of the fans' approval.

The young man clowning around in left field didn't give the impression of someone on the verge of a life-altering decision. Neither did he seem like a man on a deep journey in search of God.

"I never saw the religious side of Les," says Murray Costello. "His decision to go into the priesthood came like an absolute jolt."

If Costello was feeling disillusioned or frustrated by life in hockey, he didn't make much of an effort to share it with his family and friends. Rita Hogan remembers one of the rare times he opened up. "It all sounds glamorous," he said. "There's practice, games and some guys have girlfriends. And all I can think is 'what's this all about?'"

Just as his siblings had no idea that he was considering a dramatic lifestyle change, neither did his fellow teammates. Fellow Leaf Johnny McCormack, who had just returned to hockey after a failed attempt at the seminary, says Costello never quizzed him about his experience as a postulant. The only two people who may have been privy to these thoughts were his mother and local rector Father Francis Murray. The priests of this era tended to be men who kept their distance from the working-class pursuits of their parishioners. Father Murray, however, was an active sportsman and a regular player on the local curling teams. Murray's influence on Costello was clear: when Les was ordained, Father Murray was standing at his side.

The history of the Church is filled with dramatic conversions from otherwise worldly men and women. In fact, the best-selling religious book of the era was one such journey – Thomas Merton's *The Seven Storey Mountain*, published in 1948. Merton's book has remained a continual bestseller among post-war Catholics. The young intellectual poet from New York's Columbia University had been an atheist with no religious background whatsoever. His decision to join the Trappists – a religious community committed to living in almost primitive conditions – was seen as such a dramatic rejection of the materialist world that Merton became something of a counter-cultural hero to generations of young Catholics.

Merton, like Costello, initially kept his longing for the priesthood a secret:

My priestly ordination was, I felt, the one great secret for which I had been born. Ten years before I was ordained, when I was in the world and seemed to be one of the men in the world most unlikely to become a priest, I had suddenly realized that for me ordination to the priesthood was, in fact, a matter of life or death, heaven or hell. As I finally came within sight of this perfect meeting with the inscrutable will of God, my vocation became clear. It was mercy and a secret which were so perfectly mine that at first I intended to speak of them to no one.

The Seven Storey Mountain fits the classic format of Catholic biography. Merton's journey from atheist to Trappist monk was an updating of a familiar tale that went back to the days of St. Augustine and St. Francis – a suitably rambunctious youth, followed by a deep spiritual crisis leading to a rejection of worldly glamour and a dramatic decision to give up everything in the service of God.

Was Costello undergoing such a "crisis" in the summer of 1950? The fans in the Hollinger bleachers could easily see the man passionately engaged in the flesh-and-blood world around him, but no one glimpsed a despairing struggle of whether to choose the world or God. Unlike the tortured young Merton, Costello didn't seem to be wrestling with the notion of "conversion" or "rejection" of worldly fame. Rather, he seems to have spent the summer of 1950 wondering whether the time had simply come to move on. When his family later pressed him to say what caused him to enter the seminary, he explained that he heard a voice that simply said, "I think you should try."

In late August 1950, Les was scheduled to head back to St. Catharines for the Leaf training camp. His younger brother Murray had just signed with the Black Hawks and was heading down to his first training camp at North Bay. The two brothers hopped in to Les's Mercury for what Murray thought was a mutual drive to the big leagues.

On their way south, Les turned to Murray and said, "I'm not going to go."

Murray was shocked.

"What the hell are you going to do, Les?"

He said, "I'm going to go back to school."

"For what?"

"To be a priest. I'm going to go to the seminary."

Murray was floored. "Anyone can be a priest, Les. You play for the Toronto Maple Leafs. Are you nuts?" (Seven years later, as Les was being ordained to the priesthood, 23-year-old Murray Costello decided to hang up his own skates on a very promising hockey career and go back to school.)

Les dropped Murray off at the Black Hawks' training camp and drove on to Toronto – not to the Gardens but to St. Augustine's Seminary. All the way down he was telling himself that all he had to do was to give it a try.

One time, while doing a story on Conn Smyth, I called Father Costello.

"I'm doing a story, Father, on Conn Smythe," I began.

Costello cut me off. "Too busy to talk now, Miller," he said, hanging up.

A few days later, I saw Costello at a local coffee shop. I brought up the Smythe story.

"Remember, Father, the other day on the phone, we were talking about Conn Smythe."

"No," Costello replied. "You were talking about Smythe. I wasn't."

—*William Miller, Timins sportswriter*

Costello's decision to leave a pro hockey career and enter the seminary has always generated speculation. Part of the interest lies in the fact that Costello seems to have kept the highlights of this inner journey private.

Costello never looked upon his pro hockey days as anything special or romantic. Later in life he never took part in any "glory days" reminiscences with hockey fans and former players. When Maple Leaf Gardens was being closed in 1999, Costello was invited to be part of the final ceremonies. To the shock of the people around him, Costello said he wasn't interested.

Pat Hannigan, who eventually left hockey and ended up working with Latin American refugees, says Costello treated hockey as a game while reserving his real passion for changing the world.

"When he left hockey, he left it totally. He never spoke about his days in the NHL. What excited him was talking about helping the poor. This was what was important to him."

7. The Door Swings Both Ways

"I grew up on the Aunor Mine property and remember Les Costello when he worked on the Aunor beach crew [during his seminary years] with Johnny McLellan. I came from a family of seven boys and my mother would always bake apple pies. She'd leave the apple pies out on the window ledge to cool and when she'd come back to get them she'd always be one short. Les and Johnny would get a ladder and make off with the other apple pie."

—*Rick Young*

Connie Smythe was a pussycat compared to the black-robed rectors of St. Augustine's Seminary. The monsignors in charge of Toronto's other elite training camp weren't in the business of admitting cocky young turks to the lineup. The ones that did get in tended to be weeded out in no short order.

"The door swings both ways," Monsignor Dobel reminded the eager candidates coming through the doors of St. Augustine's every fall. It was the seminary's job to fulfill the biblical promise to separate the "wheat from the chaff." The rules were harsh and at times arbitrary: no talking in the halls, no secular newspapers, only two trips into the city a year, no friendships allowed. The seminarians were continually reminded that they must treat all fellow seminarians with the same regard. Any two seminarians becoming too chummy would be told to cool it. Although it was never mentioned, the seminary was certainly on the lookout for any sign of homosexual inclination. A seminarian who visited another seminarian in his room would be tossed out of the program.

The arbitrary power of the rector wasn't questioned. The seminary was a boot camp turning pious young men into the walking representation of 2,000 years of Catholic tradition. To the faithful, the priest was the presence of Christ himself on earth. For the Church hierarchy, these young men were expected to fulfill the Church's mission to bind on earth what would remain bound in heaven.

This power to bind and to loose was firmly linked to the belief in a strict hierarchical line of Church authority culminating in the primacy of the pope. This unquestioned power of the Bishop of Rome was a relatively recent phenomenon – an outgrowth of the First Vatican Council in 1870. Centralizing power in the Vatican had been the Church's defensive response to the rise of secular nationalism in Europe. Vatican I's attempt to codify Rome's control over the European bishops was interrupted by the invasion of the Papal States by Italian troops. Even though the pope and cardinals had been forced to flee the Vatican, the centralizing control over the European Church continued. The process was known as "ultramontane" – coined by the French Church to refer to the "beyond the mountains" influence of Rome.

Although the English-Canadian Church was far removed from the politics of Europe, it was deeply influenced by ultramontane spirituality, a world view that stressed a simple, devotional faith for the laity with unquestioning obedience to a very clear hierarchical command structure.

In post-war suburban Toronto, St. Augustine's was the training ground for this spirituality. The fear of secular influences was a dominant mark of the training. Priests were not to watch movies or to engage in the world of the laity. Ecumenism was considered a threat to the spirituality of the one true Church – a view defined by two Vatican encyclicals, *Mortalium animos* [On Religious Unity] (1928) and *Humani generis* [Concerning Some False Opinions] (1950).

Les Costello entered St. Augustine's in the fall of 1950. It was a seven-year road to ordination – a three-year philosophy degree at the University of Toronto followed by four years of theological training. Given Les's reputation and his free-spirited personality, the odds didn't appear to be in his favour. He came into the seminary as the same carefree character who had battled his way through Pittsburgh and the Leafs' organization.

Father M.J. Scully had been in the seminary for four years when Costello arrived. He was impressed by Les's ability to stick out the tough regimen. "Les was a pretty independent guy when he came to the seminary. It must have been hard for him to buckle down to the very strict discipline."

Les began his philosophy studies at St. Mary's, a residence for seminarians. Father William Kerr, the rector at St. Mary's, helped inspire the intellectual part of Les – a side that was mostly unknown to his friends from the hockey world. Costello did well in the world of academia and philosophy.

In his efforts to succeed at the seminary, Les did not fall into the trap of donning the ill-fitting costume of an overt piety. He remained the same high-spirited, fast-talking character with an underlying rebel's streak. He was also a very good judge of how to push the limits without incurring a penalty.

The one memorable time that Costello ran afoul of the seminary hierarchy occurred, not surprisingly, while he was on the ice. Organized sport was the one worldly pursuit the rectors encouraged. The seminary maintained hockey, baseball and basketball leagues. In fact, St. Augustine's had such a large pool of seminarians that it boasted three leagues of hockey – senior, junior and beginners.

The teams played on the single outdoor rink on the seminary grounds. It was rare for the rink to have proper ice until after the Christmas break and, with the often fickle Toronto weather, the seminarians were lucky to have three full weeks or a month of good ice time.

In his first year, Les hooked up with two other seminarians fresh out of the junior hockey leagues of Thunder Bay – Art Harris and Bill Fenelon. The three of them were firmly entrenched in the senior seminary league as a high-flying squad. Les approached seminary hockey the way he approached all his games. During one senior league game he tangled with fellow seminarian Ted Gravel. Both were good hockey players. Both had tempers. Words were exchanged and the gloves were dropped. It may have been a typical game for Costello and Gravel, but it wasn't typical behaviour at St. Augustine's.

That night as the seminarians gathered for the daily five o'clock spiritual reflection, Monsignor Ingoldsby called both men to step forward.

"We will not have fighting among our seminarians. It's disgraceful. Mr. Costello and Mr. Gravel are suspended from hockey for the next three weeks."

M.J. Scully recalls that, given the poor ice conditions, the three-week banishment was like being kicked out for the season.

After the sentence was read out, one of the seminarians came up to Les to offer his condolences.

"Oh well," shrugged Les. "That's the way the ball bounces."

By the time the suspension was lifted, the ice was covered in melting water. M.J. Scully vividly remembers Les Costello skating around in this slush with a hockey stick and a puck.

"He had gone from professional hockey to playing on this rinky-dink seminary team," recalls Scully. "I always admired the way he handled himself in this incident."

Many seminarians barely coped through the seven-year program and yet Costello, of all people, seemed to flourish. He found the atmosphere challenging and was clearly inspired by the spirit of his fellow seminarians.

"I came from a dog-eat-dog world," he told a television interviewer in 1980. "When I came to the seminary and found guys willing to do things for each other without any reason behind it, this impressed me. I stuck around and the next thing I knew the bishop was laying his hands on me."

The Aunor Mine has good toilers
To fix the light and fill the boilers
But the brightest of all within their reach
Are the boys that labour on the beach.

—excerpt from Les Costello's 1954 poem
for the Aunor Beach Crew

At the end of his first year in the seminary, Les was back in the Porcupine. And just like previous summers, he returned to his old position with the Combines. People still talk about the time Costello was faced with missing the train back to the seminary because of a tense ninth-inning showdown. Costello came to bat, hit a home run and rushed off in the nick of time to board the Toronto-bound train. This was to be the pattern of his life over the next number of years. In addition to batting a baseball around Hollinger Park, he picked up a summer job working on the beach crew at the Aunor Gold Mine.

The Aunor, one of a number of gold mines on the Porcupine "backroad," overlooked beautiful McDonald Lake. Les worked the beach crew with childhood friend Johnny McLellan, who would later coach the Toronto Maple Leafs. The crew was given the task of painting swings and picking up beach rubbish. In short, they didn't bend themselves out of shape about the state of the working world. While the rest of the gold mine's staff had to account for every tonne blasted and every round drilled, Costello's beach crew took a more relaxed view of the value of human labour.

"Harold Shantz was the purchasing agent for the Aunor mine," says Rick Young. "He was also in charge of the Aunor Beach. Father Les and the boys had it worked out that the minute Harold got in his car to go down to the beach to check up on things, Tony Poulin, who worked in the gatehouse, would call ahead and say, 'He's on his way.' They were always caught working."

In a tongue-and-cheek tribute to his fellow beach bums, Les Costello wrote a poem for the Aunor "Lads" who "toil beneath the sun and rain."

The benches please each shapely queen
They're Chinese red and island green
The Sea-blue tables never fail
To hold a dozen Black Horse Ale.

But even here as a genial ne'er-do-well, Les Costello revealed his underlying contemplative nature. At nine-thirty every morning, Les put down his paintbrush and disappeared into the surrounding forest. He was always gone for a full hour, gatekeeper Tony Poulin covering his exit. Les never told anyone where he was going or what he was doing, but he carried his prayer book with him.

This contemplative side had been revealed by his daily chapel visits at St. Mike's. It would remain a part of his life as a priest. And just as he did around the Aunor Beach crew, Costello kept this aspect of his life as hidden as possible.

"He was always very private in his spirituality," recalls Father Des O'Connor. "When I was with him at Nativity parish he always spent time praying before the Blessed Sacrament."

In later years, when he was pastor of St. Alphonsus parish, he often prayed before the Sacrament in the empty church. But as soon as someone came in, Les would invariably get up and head back into the rectory.

As a priest, Les Costello was known for a spirituality that was very much based on the practical works of mercy. But at the same time, he maintained a very private contemplative spirituality. This faith was firmly rooted in the devotional faith of his youth.

"He had a rugged vocation," explains Father M.J. Scully. "It was a faith very much based in the pious upbringing he had with his parents. He carried that same sense of piety throughout his life."

A reflection of this seemingly simple Irish piety was his belief in the power of the intercession of the saints. Catholics all over the world regularly read devotional pamphlets on the lives of the saints. Not only did the lives of the saints offer an instructive path for the faithful, but saints also had the power to intercede for people. One saint who struck a deep chord in Les Costello was Martin de Porres. The cult of Martin de Porres was promoted by Irish mission priests out of Dublin, Ireland.

St. Martin "of the Poor," a half-breed son of a Spanish "gentleman" and a local Indian woman, was born in Lima in 1579, when Spanish adventurers were pillaging the Native lands of Peru. Martin's dark skin pushed him outside the rigid caste system of the Spanish ruling class. The outcast bastard joined the Dominicans as a lay brother and quickly established a reputation as a great worker among the poor.

One time, it is said, St. Martin brought a naked beggar into the monastery. The man's body was covered with open sores. Martin placed the man in his own bed and nursed him back to health. The other monks were very disturbed by the fact that such a dirty and sick man had been brought inside the monastery walls.

When challenged by one of the Dominicans, St. Martin replied: "Compassion, my dear Brother, is preferable to cleanliness. Reflect that with a little soap I can easily clean my bed covers, but even with a torrent of tears I would never wash from my soul the stain that my harshness toward the unfortunate would create."

Les Costello identified with St. Martin and dreamed of leaving Canada to join the missions. It is interesting to note that St. Martin, despite all the works of mercy he carried out among his own people, also dreamt of becoming a missionary. This dream was never realized. Little did Costello know that, like St. Martin, he would have to settle for mission work among his own people.

On May 31, 1957, Les Costello was ordained to the priesthood at his home parish in South Porcupine. Many of his hockey pals came up for the occasion. Flem MacKell helped serve at Costello's first Mass. Local sportswriter Doug McLellan wrote a glowing tribute to the short pro career of Costello.

"Les lived like a King," wrote McLellan, "but yesterday morning, Les Costello became Father Les Costello in St. Joachim's parish in South Porcupine. And now all the thrills which he enjoyed through his hockey career, the Stanley Cup, the Memorial Cup twice, and all the glamour that went with the trophies have been eclipsed for Father Costello."

McLellan concluded his tribute by stating, "And so this closes the book on Les Costello."

As if.

II: God's Favourite Rebel

"Father Les asked me one time to go and find the answer to this question. 'Why are some people not given the gift of faith?' I went to find the answer and I finally asked Bishop Henry. He replied, 'Not everyone is given the gift of faith, but God gives everyone enough grace for their salvation.' Costello thought this was a perfect answer."

—*Dan Bagley, former priest*

8. On the Mile of Gold

"*After ordination, Les took Mom back home to the Valley. It was important to her to take him home because there is something special about an Irish mother with a priest for a son. People in Killaloe would kneel down right there on the street when they saw him coming because they wanted to get the blessing of the newly ordained priest. This really left an impression on Les.*"

—Murray Costello

One time the Holy Name hockey team was going up to South Porcupine for a tournament and were worried they wouldn't be able to get any beer. They went to Father Les and asked him if he knew a place in South Porcupine where they'd be able to get some.

He gave them an address and said, "Knock on the door and tell the woman that answers that Father Les said to give as much beer as these boys want."

The boys went to South Porcupine and dutifully went to the house and said what Father Les had told them to say.

The woman responded, "Why does my son always do stuff like this?"

—Kirkland Lake story

Rita and Les Costello on Commercial Avenue in South Porcupine, circa 1932.
(Photo courtesy of Mrs. Rita [Costello] Hogan.)

The three older Costello children: Rita, Les and baby Murray.
(Photo courtesy of Mrs. Rita [Costello] Hogan.)

Les Costello (fourth from left, second row) with Golden Avenue Public School hockey team. Mr. Don Simpson is the teacher/coach.
(Photo courtesy of Mrs. Rita [Costello] Hogan.)

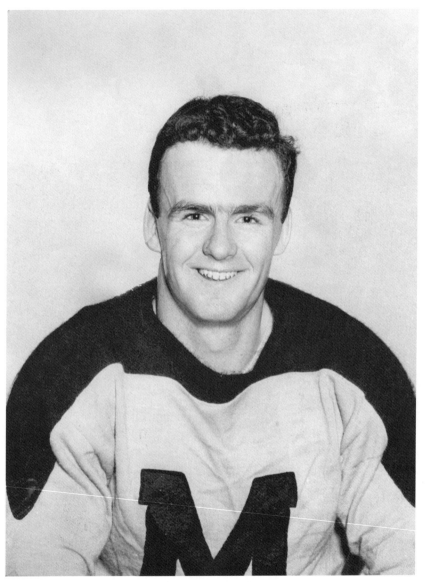

Les Costello as a player on the St. Mike's Majors.
(Photo courtesy of Mrs. Rita [Costello] Hogan.)

Les Costello (second from left, second row) with the Pittsburg Hornets, 1949–1950.
(Photo courtesy of Mrs. Rita [Costello] Hogan.)

Les Costello in uniform with the Toronto Maple Leafs.
(Photo is from the Imperial Oil–Turofsky/Hockey Hall of Fame collection and is courtesy of the
Hockey Hall of Fame, Toronto, www.hhof.com.)

Les Costello (at left) with Bill Barilko (centre) and Howie Meeker (right).
(Photo is from the Imperial Oil–Turofsky/Hockey Hall of Fame collection and is courtesy of the
Hockey Hall of Fame, Toronto, www.hhof.com.)

Les Costello with his mother, Claire, before leaving for the seminary, fall 1950.
(Photo courtesy of Mrs. Rita [Costello] Hogan.)

3 golfing brothers 1955

Les Costello golfs with his brothers Murray (left) and Jack (centre), during a summer break from the seminary in 1955.
(Photo courtesy of Mrs. Rita [Costello] Hogan.)

Les Costello being ordained at St. Joachim's parish in South Porcupine, May 31, 1957. Les Costello and Father Francis Murray, followed by parish priest Father Pensineault and Canon Jones. Mr. and Mrs. Costello are kneeling in the first row. (Photo courtesy of Mrs. Rita [Costello] Hogan.)

Les Costello offering up his first Mass, with NHL player Flem MacKell helping serve Mass, 1957. (Photo courtesy of Mrs. Rita [Costello] Hogan.)

Les Costello as a young ordained priest, 1957.
(Photo courtesy of Mrs. Rita [Costello] Hogan.)

Father Les Costello enjoys a cigar and a copy of *The Homiletic and Pastoral Review* during his short and turbulent stay at Blessed Sacrament parish in Noranda, Quebec, 1961. (Photo courtesy of Mrs. Rita [Costello] Hogan.)

A Flying Fathers souvenir program. (Courtesy of the Hockey Hall of Fame collection.)

First game of the Flying Fathers, North Bay, 1963. (from left to right): CHCH radio hosts Greg Lawrence and Terry Spearen, Father Les Costello, Father Bernard Pappin and Father Brian McKee.
(Photo courtesy of the North Bay Nugget.)

Father Les Costello with Rolly the Clown and Father O'Connor at the Timmins Winter Carnival, February 1968. (Photo courtesy of Mrs. Rita [Costello] Hogan.)

The Flying Fathers in the early 1980s. (on ice): Dan Bagley, Father Scanlan, Father Dennis Kennelly. (back row): seminarian Billy Brennan, Father Mike Grace, Father Les Costello, Father Al Love, Father Grant Neville, M.J. Blimkie, Ernie Smith, trainer (unknown). (Photo: *Toronto Star* archives.)

Father Costello conducting a baptism at St. Alphonsus parish.
(Photo courtesy of Mrs. Rita [Costello] Hogan.)

Father Costello with children at a family baptism.
(Photo courtesy of Mrs. Rita [Costello] Hogan.)

Father M.J. Scully speaking at the opening of the Father Les Costello Arena, Cobalt, Ontario, in August 2003. (Photo courtesy of the author.)

The Costello family at the opening of the arena. From left to right: Murray Costello, Corinne Ivancic (daughter of Don Costello), Rita (Costello) Hogan, and Jack Costello. (Photo courtesy of the author.)

L es Costello was ordained into a Church that had seen little change in generations. Author Bernard Daly, in his book *Beyond Secrecy: The Untold Story of Canada and the Second Vatican Council,* writes:

> If Samuel de Champlain could have walked into a 1950s Catholic Church, he would have felt pretty much at home: the priest at the altar with his back to the people, the Latin, the incense, the sanctuary bells. There was something awesome about being part of a culture that seemed to stand outside time. It was also somewhat unreal.

Costello was ordained into a Church that understood its mission as eternal and unchangeable. The authority of the priest extended through a strict hierarchical lineage through the bishops, cardinals, the pope and then, by extension, back to Christ himself. "You are the rock," Christ told Peter, "And upon this Rock I will build my church." Rocks didn't change with the seasons. They didn't adapt. The power of the rock was its ability to withstand pressure and force. After all, was this not what Christ wanted when he commanded, "The Gates of Hell will not prevail against thee" (Matthew 16:18-20)? Little wonder church leaders looked upon innovation as a threat to the very will of God.

At the time of Costello's ordination, however, Italian Cardinal Angelo Roncalli was openly questioning whether the centralized bureaucracy that had grown under Pope Pius XII was stifling the spirit of the Church. In a memorable speech to the College of Cardinals, Roncalli attacked the premise that the authority of the Church was beyond question or change:

> Authoritarianism suffocates truth, reducing everything to a rigid and empty formalism that is dependent on outside discipline. It curbs wholesome initiative, mistakes hardness for firmness, inflexibility for dignity. Paternalism is a caricature of true fatherliness. It is often accompanied by an unjustifiable proprietary attitude to one's victim, a habit of intruding, a lack of proper respect for the rights of subordinates.

Within a year, Pius was dead and the 77-year-old Roncalli had been elected to take his place. He announced to the world that it was time to throw open the windows of the Church to let the light in and to allow church leaders to look out. Nothing would ever be the same again.

"It was Thanksgiving weekend, 1962. A friend and I had hitchhiked to Noranda for the weekend to see my girlfriend. We headed home on Monday and got a ride as far as Kenogami. We were standing by the side of the road with our thumbs out when two cars raced by us heading north, going well over the speed limit. The car in the lead put on its brakes and pulled over way down the road, did a power turn and pulled up in front of us.

Father Les rolled down the window and said, 'Jump in, Tim! There's a case of beer for whoever gets to South End first!'

We left big black stripes on the pavement as we took off. Unfortunately, that stop cost Les a case of beer. But he dropped me off at home, making sure I gave his best to my parents, then headed home to celebrate Thanksgiving with his folks. That was pure Father Les."

—Tim Miner

Les Costello had gone into the seminary with the dream of a mission posting, but the Church refused to let him leave the diocese. Bishop Maxime Tessier chose instead to send him to the neighbouring gold-mining town of Kirkland Lake. At the time, the Timmins diocese spread over 300 kilometres (from Cochrane in the north to Latchford in south, including the English-speaking population of Rouyn-Noranda, Quebec). The diocese was largely francophone, with the English-speaking parishes spread out along a mix of culturally diverse communities – conservative farming towns, isolated francophone logging communities and the multi-ethnic mining towns.

Kirkland Lake was known for its famed "Mile of Gold" – seven operating gold mines all within a stone's throw of the town's downtown corridor. Holy Name parish was one street over from the main drag of Government Road.

As was the case in every parish he went to, Costello quickly established a reputation at the parish and, indeed, all over town. "He came in like a ball of fire," was how one cleric remembers the Costello invasion. Younger working families saw him as a breath of fresh air. Older people were shocked by his rough-talking manner and seemingly irreverent behaviour – such as hopping over the communion rail on his way up to the altar.

"My mother used to be aghast at his antics," recalls Frank Quinn, who first met Fr. Les in Timmins. "He'd come over to the house, throw off his collar and say in front of my mother, 'Go steal a dime out of your mother's purse and we'll bet on whether or not Beliveau will score the next goal.'"

Costello's lineage as an ex-Leaf certainly added to his appeal with the younger generation. He was constantly down at the arena encouraging both the local Catholic and Protestant kids to get out on the ice and play. Costello played against the local kids with the same rough-housing style he employed in the major leagues. But there was one noticeable difference. The NHL had been ruthless in its pursuit of the winners, whereas Costello insisted that the local games be open to all kids, regardless of their speed or skill. Even though he was a natural "winner," he never forgot the beauty of pond shinny where every kid had an equal chance to shine, and where fun was more important than victory.

"I don't know how he managed to balance the competitiveness of playing hard with making sure that people who couldn't play well were looked out for," recalls Rita (Costello) Hogan. "But he didn't approve of all-star teams or picking out the best players. He wanted every kid to have the chance to get out and play."

Kirkland Lake was a tightly knit community, but like all mining towns, it was a place where people easily fell through the cracks. The economy of hardrock mining was dependent on a steady influx of hungry young men willing to take a chance on the dangerous work underground. Some made it and some didn't. The mining economy chewed its way through the health and stability of families just as it chewed through the gold-bearing rock veins. Gold mining had appalling rates of injuries and deaths as well as industrial disease. Lung cancers, silicosis and emphysema were part of the fabric of life in hardrock mining communities. Up to the 1950s, for example, the average life expectancy of an Eastern European man was a mere 41 years of age.

The hodge-podge boarding houses and rented-out rooms above the local beer parlours were full of folks who had been washed up and left on the rocky hills of Kirkland Lake.

There were no soup kitchens, food banks or even an organized St. Vincent de Paul Society – an organization that is active in most dioceses across Canada to serve the needs of the local poor. Thus the rectory door became the number-one choice for many folks in trouble. Bright-eyed young clerics, fresh out of the seminary, quickly found that serving the poor was a rough road. Few priests had any real-world experience. Once assigned to a parish, they found themselves having to work through heartbreaking stories of damaged lives and abusive families at a time when social service agencies were minimal.

The Catholic Church had a long history of social action in the service of the poor. Many of the great religious orders had been founded on a commitment to poverty and social justice. A young priest like Costello would have grown up on the stories of the saints that stressed the obligation to give selflessly to the poor.

Costello threw himself into serving the needs of the town's underclass. If a family lacked clothes, Costello found clothes. If their children had no beds or dressers, he found furniture. And like his hero St. Martin, he didn't believe the rectory should be off limits to the needs of the poor.

Costello was an assistant to Canon Harold Jones. (The term "canon" was an honourary designation for priests who had reached a certain level of service in the diocese. A canon was technically considered an assistant to the bishop.) The mild-mannered Jones had maintained a dignified order to the rectory – an order that Costello soon reduced to shambles. Hockey sticks piled up in the doorway, bags of food and clothes gathered in the hall. An endless stream of people kept Costello going to all hours of the night.

"He [Costello] is the cross God sent me to bear," Jones once told a parishioner when the two priests were sharing Nativity parish in Timmins. "I don't get to sleep. People are knocking on the doors at all hours of the day and night. When I get up in the morning, I never know who will be sleeping in the office."

Despite their differences, however, the two men quickly grew to appreciate one another. Jones couldn't help but respond to Costello's irrepressible zeal for life, and Costello was inspired by Jones's intellect.

"Les really loved Canon Jones," says Father Des O'Connor. "He'd say, 'If you can't get along with Jonesy there's got to be something wrong with you.'"

Costello loved games, competition and betting. On trips to the city he would always drag straitlaced priests with him to the betting tracks. During evening meals at the rectory, Costello set up a game that all visiting clerics had to play – "Stump Jonesy." The object was to throw out a line of poetry and see if Canon Jones, who had a fantastic memory and was extremely well read, could identify the author. Priests who weren't fans of Frost, Service or Yeats found this game tedious, but Costello treated the poetry challenge with the same zest he had for playing the horses. The game was typical Costello. He could make any mundane activity into a source of challenge.

"Come on, Des," he'd say to Father O'Connor as they were waiting near a bank of elevators. "Let's bet a buck to see which elevator comes first.'"

Jones's intellect provided sermons that were careful, reflective and measured. Costello, on the other hand, sermonized in the same rat-a-tat-tat speaking style of his general conversation – fast, punchy and straight to the point. When the two priests were working at Nativity parish, the bishop brought in new rules regarding Christmas donations to the clergy. Families often made cash donations to the priests at Christmas time. But a change in diocesan rules meant that any money that was not specifically made out in a priest's name had to be handed over to the diocese.

At the first Sunday Mass, Canon Jones tried to explain this change in rules. In his halting and careful tone, he left many parishioners wondering exactly was being changed. Costello, at the next Mass, made it much simpler.

"If yiz don't make the cheque out to us, the money goes to the bishop," he said from the pulpit. "So there's only two things ya really need to know about this issue – when you sign the cheque, it's Costello with two l's and Jones with a J."

Costello's time in Kirkland Lake was relatively short – a three-year "apprenticeship." And yet, as would be the case in each of the towns where he served, stories of Costello's time there would remain fresh in local memory long after he was moved elsewhere.

9. The Noranda Alouettes

"I remember when Father Les joined the hockey team from Noranda. It killed people here [the Porcupine] that this English priest went and joined a Quebec team. When the team came to play here, people booed and booed. He didn't care. I think he scored two goals."

—George Stefanic, Schumacher resident

In 1961, Les Costello was moved over to Blessed Sacrament parish in Noranda, Quebec. The move was part of a typical training process for a young priest. Although across the provincial border, the large English-speaking population in Noranda was administered by the Timmins diocese. Up until the Parti Québécois victory in 1976, the mining region of northwestern Quebec – Rouyn-Noranda, Malartic and Val d'Or – was very much part of the cultural family of the mining towns of northeastern Ontario.

Like other mining towns, Rouyn-Noranda was a deliberately stratified community under the ever-watchful eye of Noranda Mines. Noranda was a company town, with Noranda Mines owning all the services and houses. This company town served as an enclave for the English-speaking minority. The larger francophone majority, along with many of the immigrant families, was relegated to the poorer apartment blocks and boarding houses of neighbouring Rouyn.

As in Kirkland Lake, Costello's reputation as the hockey-playing priest preceded him. Cliff Connolly, who grew up in Noranda, remembers the initial split in the congregation over this brash young priest.

"Whenever Father Costello was around there were no empty seats at Mass. But there were still a lot of people who didn't think what he was doing was proper."

One person who shared this view was Father John Caulfield. It was not that Caulfield objected to Costello's sports inclinations. As a former champion amateur boxer, Father Caulfield had always maintained parish-based youth clubs and hockey teams. But Caulfield never strayed from a belief that the priest had to be somehow separate from the lives of his working-class parishioners.

Costello, however, was always down at the arena, playing pickup hockey with the miners or organizing local youth. One time a woman phoned the rectory to speak with Father Costello. "Oh, I'm sorry, dear lady," replied Father Caulfield. "If you want to speak to Father Costello you have to phone the Noranda Recreation Centre."

Costello never felt comfortable in Father Caulfield's house and often ate his meals at a boardinghouse down the road. It didn't help that Caulfield's sister was the housekeeper at the rectory. She didn't approve of Costello and carried on a little tit-for-tat war with the roughneck clergyman. One time, she threw his skates down the stairs.

"Don't touch my fuckin' skates again," Costello told her as he was going out the door. When he returned, he found she had thrown pennies all over his room. He thought this was hilarious.

Cliff Connolly thinks the difficulties between Costello and Caulfield were part of a generational war between two very strong-willed clerics.

"I don't think Father Caulfield had any idea about what Costello was doing. Father Caulfield was very religious, but I think he was a little jealous of all the attention that Costello had."

One time Father Caulfield approached Cliff's father, Owen, who was head of the parish council. Caulfield expressed his concerns about Costello.

Owen shrugged. "Let him continue on the road he's going. He's obviously doing something right."

Father Caulfield later confided to Father Scully that he had to admire Les Costello's inner spirituality.

"He might come in at four in the morning," Caulfield had stated. "And he might put his feet up on the pews [an action Caulfield saw as scandalous], but he always spends time in front of the Blessed Sacrament."

Costello was a good friend of Anglican rector Jack Watson, of the nearby All Saints Church. The two used to sit in Watson's office sharing smokes, shots of rye and belly laughs. Both clerics were active in minor hockey and Costello became a regular face among the Anglican parishioners.

Costello was also a regular face in the poor tenements of Rouyn. And he didn't work alone – he drummed up volunteers to accompany him on his visits to needy families. In most churches, the average parishioner was able to take comfort in the fact that their obligation for charity tended to be delivered through a safe intermediary – an organization or mission. Such donations ensured that direct interaction with the poor was almost non-existent.

And yet, throughout the first half of the twentieth century, a growing movement in the Church encouraged lay people to become directly involved in the works of the gospel. Dorothy Day's Catholic Worker movement and Catherine Doherty's Madonna House apostolate were two lay organizations that moved "charity" into a larger realm of radical solidarity with the urban underclass. Costello was, in his own way, moving the good parishioners of Blessed Sacrament and of All Saints Anglican into a deeper dialogue of faith. These families lived a facade of English civility in what was still a very rough northern smelter town. Through their volunteer work with Costello, many of these people were touched by the direct experience of poverty.

Laura (Kruger) Landers remembers going with her father, a member of All Saints, on a furniture drive into the poorer streets of Rouyn. "My first real glimpse of what it was like to be poor was when I was with my dad on one of his deliveries for Father Costello and saw the conditions of this one apartment in Rouyn."

This woman told me that she knew Father Les and tried to help him with his charity.

"As a matter of fact," she said, "just a few months ago we left a sofa for him in our driveway."

I said, "Why would you put a sofa in your driveway in this kind of weather?"

"We didn't want him to come into our house."

"Oh, and why would that be?"

"Well," she said, "we knew if we let him into our living room he'd say, 'The sofa's fine, but those two end tables are getting kind of worn and that lamp doesn't look good.'"

—*Murray Costello*

Another noticeable factor in Costello's ministry was his casual disregard for private property. Costello thought nothing of hitting up well-off parishioners for money to buy cigarettes for local prisoners. During a visit to the Connolly family at Christmas, he noticed they had two bottles of wine on the shelf.

"I'll take one of these," he said, to the shock of his hosts. "I'm going to visit the nuns and they have nothing."

In the history of the Church there has always been a so-called primitive communism based on the description laid out in the Acts of the Apostles that "those who believed were together and had all things in common; and they began to sell their possessions and were sharing them with all, as anyone might have need."

Historical figures such as St. Francis and St. Benedict saw the communal sharing of property as a fundamental part of Catholic social obligations. The tradition is expressed by the fourteenth-century Benedictine writer St. Gertrude, who stated that "property, the more common it becomes, the more holy it becomes."

Costello was aware of the radical nature of this gospel call, but he was also able to draw on the tradition of sharing that had existed among the families he had known as a child in South Porcupine.

"He was a very strong believer in people giving back to the community something of which they'd received," explains Father Des O'Connor. "There was a hockey player who had done very well and Les asked him for help. The man replied he didn't have time. Les just couldn't understand this lack of generosity."

> *So this priest is in the shower after a hockey game and he's wearing his underwear. One of the guys says, "Father, why are you wearing your underwear in the shower?"*
>
> *The priest replies, "I hate looking down on the unemployed."*
>
> —*Father Costello joke*

Not long after arriving at Blessed Sacrament, Costello was being courted by the Noranda Alouettes – one of the best Senior A hockey teams in the country. That year they had won the coveted Northern Ontario Hockey Association championship. Bishop Tessier, like Father Caulfield, wasn't pleased by the prospect of having Costello join the Alouettes. Tessier finally relented but not before imposing a number of restrictions, such as the rule that Costello had to leave the game five minutes before it ended so as to not share the shower with the other players.

Costello had already played once for the Noranda Alouettes. While he was stationed at Holy Name parish in Kirkland Lake, Costello had been asked to augment Noranda's lineup during a particularly tense playoff game. Costello's schedule at the church made it impossible to get to the game on time. In response, Noranda Mines sent their private jet to ferry Costello to and from the game.

Local hockey fans were ecstatic at his decision to join the team for a full season. Cliff Connolly, a star player on the Alouettes, remembers the prowess Costello brought to the team.

"I was aware of his reputation when he came to Noranda, but I had no idea what kind of hockey player he was. He was a great skater. I think what held him back was he could never get into full shape because he couldn't play all the games. He was doing his priestly duties at the same time."

Was Costello's decision to join the Noranda team part of an unresolved desire to maintain the camaraderie and excitement of the pro-hockey life?

Connolly doesn't think so.

"He always put his role as a priest above the game. Father Les came in five minutes before the game and five minutes after it was done he was gone. He loved if we won but he didn't care if we lost. In those days it was very seldom that he'd come out with the team for a drink."

Costello's decision to don skates for Noranda was certainly a break with priestly tradition, but he toed the line when it came to matters of faith. Players hoping to get a reprieve to eat steak before a Friday game didn't get any slack from him – "Hey, you know the rules," he'd say.

Costello had grown up in a Church that was seemingly unchangeable – from the reciting of the Mass in Latin to the eating of fish on Fridays. And yet, during this season with Noranda, Costello's Church was set on a path of unprecedented change.

Much to the shock of church faithful and the Vatican hierarchy, Pope John XXIII convened the Second Vatican Council (1962–1965). In an atmosphere of surprising collegiality, the pope invited cardinals, bishops and religious thinkers from around the world (including those from other Christian traditions) to address the need for change in the Catholic Church. While church officials scrambled to maintain the traditions of secrecy and order over impending Vatican pronouncements, John XXIII insisted on electronic balloting and a public address system to adequately convey the perspectives of the 2,500 delegates.

He spoke of the need for *aggiornamento* – the updating of the traditions that young priests like Costello had taken as fundamental features of Catholic life. Newspaper reporters from around the world flocked to this global event. As the Council unfolded over the early 1960s, a flood of changes was announced. No longer would the priest stand with his back to the people. No longer would the Mass be said in Latin. New forms of music would be welcome, and lay participation encouraged. While the media tended to focus on the dropping of old customs, such as the "no meat on Fridays" rule, the real work of the Council involved a massive overhaul of the centralized authority of the Vatican to bring an ancient tradition into the twentieth century.

Costello's career in Senior A hockey ended at the close of the '61–62 season. He was obviously looking for a way to integrate his hockey-playing skills with his ministry, but organized hockey didn't appear to be the route to follow.

Soon after the Noranda season, Costello's teammate Cliff Connolly moved with his young family to the mill town of Témiscamingue, Quebec. Costello, who had a reputation as someone who didn't let people get close to him, developed a lifelong friendship with Connolly. When one of the Connolly children was born with a severe disability, Costello provided support. He could see the growing strain on the family as they struggled; there was no medical or social support for them in Quebec. The couple stayed up most nights trying to look after their child. One day Costello phoned out of the blue and announced he was "coming for supper." He drove 250 kilometres from Noranda to the Connolly house in Témiscamingue. The dinner was typical Costello – he came in the door ready to get right to the point.

"You can't keep going on this way," he told them. "Your son needs an institution that can look after his needs. You'll have to leave Quebec and move to Ontario where you can get medical coverage. And you have to have another child to take your mind off your loss. You have to start over as a family."

The advice given, Costello jumped in his car and drove the hilly bush roads back to Noranda. The Connollys listened to him, just as they would listen many times over the coming decades.

"When my wife died a few years ago," says Cliff Connolly, "he'd be calling me after 11 p.m. to check up and see how I was doing."

Cliff Connolly has fond memories of the glory days he spent with the Noranda Alouettes. But he has much fonder memories of his friendship with Les Costello.

"He was a helluva lot better as a priest than as a hockey player. His work in the parish always overpowered anything he ever did in hockey."

10. The Flying Fathers

"Les Costello was the whole team. He was everything. His enthusiasm made you want to get up in the morning to do what had to be done. One time I had a cold and didn't feel like doing anything. He said, 'Do you know how many times I don't feel like doing something? Get off your arse and get it done.'"

—Frank Quinn, manager, Flying Fathers

In early 1963, Les Costello was on a ski trip in Collingwood with his friends Father Brian "Buck" McKee and Father Bill Scanlan. McKee, who was stationed in North Bay, had hatched an idea for putting together a team of priests for a one-off charity hockey game against radio station CHCH. A local boy had lost an eye and McKee was looking to raise money through a benefit challenge to send the lad to Toronto for medical treatments.

Costello, with his pro-hockey background, was an obvious choice for McKee's pickup team. But so were a number of other priests. Father John Caswell, who was active on this first team, says the spirit of the early Flying Fathers had been instilled into these young men in the seminary.

"We were trained in the seminary to be team players and athletic. We were trained to go out and get things done."

The parishes were built, for better or for worse, on the individual drive and initiatives of the priest. McKee personified the best of this breed. He was tough, young and athletic. By the mid-1960s he had established an extensive charity network in the city of Sudbury.

Like Costello, McKee was a maverick with little concern for regulations or pious propriety. For example, McKee thought nothing of loading a group of teenagers into a truck to pay an unexpected visit to the rectory of a parish priest who was away on vacation. McKee announced to the startled housekeeper that the boys had come to pick up the parish priest's prized piano because it had been "donated" to the boys' camp. A week or so later the boys saw the outraged parish priest storming into McKee's office. He left empty-handed. McKee "appropriated" the piano just as he appropriated numerous other items he felt would improve the lot of the camp.

One time McKee drove to Toronto to pick up mattresses that were being donated to his charitable work. McKee loaded the mattresses on the back of his pickup and headed back up Highway 400. He was listening to the radio as a traffic reporter in a helicopter announced there was chaos on the 400 thanks to mattresses flying down the freeway. McKee looked behind him only to see the last of the mattresses flying off the back of his truck. He stopped, grabbed one or two mattresses and took off down the road ahead of the police.

A publicity photo from this February 1963 game captures the élan of these ecclesiastical leaders. The photo shows Costello, Fathers Bernard Pappin and Brian McKee facing off against CHCH radio hosts Greg Lawrence and Terry Spearen. The media team is dressed in proper hockey gear, while the Flying Fathers are decked out in simple black pants and rough pullovers.

What stands out about the photo is the brash confidence of the priests. Costello and McKee grin slyly at the camera, while Pappin (later auxiliary bishop of Sault Ste. Marie) has the brooding good looks of a matinee idol. These cocky young clerics would be unrecognizable in today's era of an aged clergy.

"Father Les Costello. Your wife wants you to call home. The baby's sick."

—typical announcement during a Flying Fathers hockey game

This charity match had been scheduled for a rink at the local air force base, but interest was so high that the event was moved to North Bay's Memorial Gardens. The game more than lived up to its hype. The priests showed off their skills both as hockey players and as comedians. They threw pies and relied on slapstick Catholic routines with impromptu confessionals for the refs and genuflecting linesmen. The crowd loved it and $3,500 was raised.

Soon McKee and Costello were getting requests for other appearances. The team played five games in its second season. A proper team logo was created to replace makeshift hockey uniforms.

"A team without its own sweaters is no team at all," Father John Caswell argued. He wanted a look – an identity that made the Flying Fathers instantly identifiable wherever they went.

Identifiable they were. The team was soon being featured in newspaper and magazine articles. They were profiled on *Front Page Challenge, Hockey Night in Canada* and *Ripley's Believe It or Not.* By 1971, the team was playing a schedule of 30-plus games a year and touring from Alaska down the west coast of the United States and across Canada.

The original lineup of the team was made up of priests including Bill Scanlon, Pete Vallely, Pat Blake and Art Appleton. Costello, however, was the driving force behind the team. Sportswriter Frank Orr described Costello's presence on the ice:

> He was like a mouse in an oxygen bottle. He just flew around out there. He never did anything half-measure and he seemed to be on the ice all game. When he wasn't, he was hollering pretty loud from the bench.

Costello thrived on the Fathers' antics of hockey speed and cornball Catholicism. They were the Harlem Globetrotters with Roman collars.

Every game featured the same mixture of clownish antics – a drag-wearing player with balloon breasts; Father Scanlan decked out in a Beatles wig to offset complaints that his bald head was emitting too much glare for the opposing players; the goonish "Flying Nun." Ernie Smith played the role of Sister Mary Shooter. His job was to spear, trip and slash the other team with his flagrant abuse of the rules. When the hapless opponents attempted to hit back they would be penalized, allowing Sister Mary the chance to carry out an outrageous penalty shot.

The slapstick routines spoke to an era when the Catholic community was still very much burdened by cultural stereotypes (such as priest-ridden "knee benders," the slur that Protestant fans would shout). As with other cultural communities (for example, American Irish, Italian and Jewish communities), a natural response was to transform these stereotypes with humour and self-deprecating subversion. Thus the image of the Fathers was defined by mixing two classic mid-twentieth-century cultural icons – the "good" priest, personified by Bing Crosby in *The Bells of St. Mary's*, and the Saturday matinee zaniness of the Three Stooges.

"The games were all scripted out and choreographed," says team manager Frank Quinn. "It was all so corny but it worked. We'd really get involved in the games and would have as many laughs as the crowd."

Estimates of the monies raised for local charities range between one and four million dollars over the 40-year career of the Fathers. Frank Quinn says that the four-million-dollar estimate is very much on the low side.

"There was one game alone in Toronto where we made a quarter of a million dollars. We played to 17,000 people in Vancouver, Calgary and Edmonton. Another year we made over $300,000 in eight or ten games."

In 1970, the Flying Fathers made their first of a number of trips overseas to play against Canadian and American forces personnel in Germany. On one of those trips they were granted an audience with the pope. Costello presented Paul VI with a hockey stick and told him it wasn't to be used for twirling spaghetti.

"The hockey is just an excuse for nonsense. This is what people come looking for. They know the priest is in church. They know he can help you if you have problems, but most of all they want to know the priest is human. After seeing us play, maybe they'll look upon their own priest as more approachable, more human."

—*Father Tim Shea, Flying Father Captain, 1981*

The Flying Fathers treated their road tours as a chance for serious mission work. In every town they played, the Flying Fathers fanned out to hospitals, schools and group homes to meet people in need. After every event they attended large parties held in church basements and community halls. Costello was always a main draw for the local fans. His fame as a hockey-playing priest had dwarfed any fame he had had during his short professional career.

"It amazed me how famous he was," recalls his friend Len Bilodeau. "One time we were on the subway in Montreal and Costello was standing there with this big straw hat, a dirty T-shirt and pants. He just started singing right there on the subway. I was so embarrassed but people were coming up to him and saying, 'Aren't you Father Costello?' They all knew him."

"It didn't matter if we were in the Arctic or on Vancouver Island," recalls long-time Flying Father Dan Bagley. "People came up to Cossie like he was their best friend."

Back in the early days of St. Mike's, Father Henry Carr had dreamed of securing a Catholic place in society by creating a team of winners. Costello and McKee turned Carr's dream upside down with a carnival on skates. But the carnival clowns exuded a rebel spirit that often bumped up against the tight confines of the Catholic Church.

Some bishops didn't want their priests to play with the Fathers because they feared this taste of freedom would lead to an exodus from the priesthood. But many young priests found a reason to stay because of the influence of priests like Costello, McKee and Scanlan.

In the 1970s, the team picked up one of its all-time legendary rebels – goalie Father Vaughan Quinn, OMI. An ex-alcoholic and long-time maverick, Quinn worked with alcoholics on the streets of Detroit. He was the subject of the 1986 TV documentary *The Mighty Quinn*. In the haunting opening sequence of the documentary, Quinn is seen driving around the streets of Detroit in his black hearse picking up alcoholics out of the alleys.

Elmore Leonard, America's king of cool *noir,* was so impressed with Vaughan Quinn, he made him a character in his book *The Touch*:

Father Vaughan Quinn...[was] a priest who played hockey and might've been a street fighter at one time. He could be a mean bugger, a hip priest with graying hair over his ears, and with the look of a guy who could tell you were bullshitting him, used to drunks lying to him, making excuses. There was a scar on his chin, from a blind-side meeting with a hockey puck, playing with the Flying Fathers.

While Elmore Leonard was profiling Quinn, Hollywood was considering a movie based on Costello's crew. The idea had come from Michael Eisner of Disney after he read about Father Costello. Eisner brought in famed director Francis Ford Coppola. The plan was to have Wayne Gretzky star as a young seminarian on a Flying Fathers team. The script was based on a classic Disney premise – the easy-going Fathers find themselves outgunned and outmatched by the mighty Russian Red Army team. In the movie's climax, the Fathers' outlandish ice antics would baffle the nasty Russians, leading to a spectacular win.

Coppola flew the main priests – Fathers Quinn, Shea, Neville and Costello – down to Tinseltown. Costello wasn't impressed. He berated the famous producer for the "immorality" of his recent smash hit, *Apocalypse Now.* A sheepish Coppola defended the film by saying it had made a lot of money.

"There are more important things in life than making money," Costello barked.

The Flying Fathers knew they were out of their league with the Hollywood heavy hitters, so they phoned the only famous person they knew – Charles Schultz (creator of the Peanuts comics) and asked him for help. Schultz had come to know the Fathers after promoting the team's tour in California. He provided a lawyer to help negotiate the film rights.

In the end, Gretzky bombed the screen test and the Fathers objected to some of Coppola's racier subplot. The movie was never made. Eisner, however, wasn't done with the hockey theme. In 1996 Disney released the hit *The Mighty Ducks*. When one considers that a lame movie like *The Mighty Ducks* resulted in the creation of a pro hockey team and a merchandizing bonanza, one wonders what the impact might have been if this Hollywood blockbuster had instead been based on the life of hero priests.

11. In the Land of Silver

"One time when we were travelling we came upon this very prestigious restaurant. Costello was dressed in his ripped-up T-shirt and shorts. He looked inside and said, 'Let's go in.'"

This place had bouncers and I said, 'They'll never let us in because of the way we're dressed.'

'Let's see how far we can get,' he said, taking a run into the restaurant.

We didn't get in at all and they grabbed us and were escorting us back out onto the street. Costello laughed and laughed."

—Len Bilodeau, St. Patrick's parishioner

"He socialized on the same level as the people did. He wasn't above the people. He was just one of the people. It didn't matter who you were. In his eyes everybody was equal."

—Gord Lapierre, St. Alphonsus parishioner

On a hot and dusty summer's day, there were only two places to escape the heat in Cobalt – working in the cold, wet drifts of the local silver mines, or diving into the spring-fed waters of Bass Lake. While the men took dubious comfort from the frigid ventilation of the underground day shift, everyone else bustled off to the beach. All day long a steady stream of kids rode their bikes along the winding highway to the lake.

Bass Lake was a summer paradise. Ball teams played in the softball grounds. Mothers sunned themselves on the grass while little ones dug imaginary cities out of wet sand. Teenagers hovered like gangly birds on the wooden dock anchored out in the deep, clear water. The dock was turf – and the boys claimed their spot on this turf by roughhousing or showing off their diving skills. If you had a message for Father Les Costello on a hot day, you'd have to swim out to the dock.

Folks still remember the day Costello decided to give a shove to Len Bilodeau, a big, strapping teenager. Bilodeau may have been a hell of a skater, but he wasn't much for swimming. He came up out of the water, choking and hacking, with fists swinging. While the beach crowd watched, Costello and Bilodeau were both escorted off the beach for scrapping.

Bilodeau and Costello became lifelong buddies, sharing a love for card games, hunting and "mixing things up." There was the time that big Rolly Bovaire, a local miner, came over to the Bilodeau home. While Bovaire was outside talking with Len's dad, Costello came up with the bright idea of tackling Bovaire.

"You hit him high and I'll hit him low," Costello suggested.

"You're crazy," Bilodeau replied. "He'll kill both of us."

Costello wasn't to be put off and convinced Bilodeau to join his scheme. The two of them came tearing down the stairs at breakneck speed. But just as Costello leapt off the bottom stair, Len stopped dead to watch the priest go crashing into the big man.

Big Rolly took the full weight of Costello's charge and then, without breaking a sweat, ran Costello straight into the nearby duck pond.

Such priestly behavior may have been shocking and unseemly in other places, but not in Cobalt. Costello had arrived there in 1966 to take charge of St. Patrick's parish as well as the neighbouring Mission of the Holy Spirit in the town of Latchford. It was his first chance at leadership of his own parish, following nine years in the "minor leagues" as an assistant cleric at other churches.

Following his rocky time under Father Caulfield, Costello had spent three years at Nativity parish in Timmins working under Monsignor Martindale. It was during this time that he began considering, once again, whether to leave the north for mission work in South America. Father Martin Jeffery of the diocese, however, convinced Costello to stay and serve the needs in the region. The bishop's decision to give Costello charge of St. Patrick's gave him the opportunity to create his own mission work in the north.

Costello's excitement about taking over St. Pat's was matched by the anticipation of the local congregation.

"It was big news that Father Les, the Flying Father, was coming to Cobalt," recalls Len Bilodeau. "His reputation as a professional hockey player was so big. The church was always full when he was here. People hated to miss Mass."

Poor indeed was the man at the coffee shop who wasn't there to witness the latest punchline zinger tossed out during a Costello sermon. The church also began to be frequented by many non-Catholics, who found his lack of pretension and down-to-earth style refreshing.

He was often seen rushing into Mass five minutes late because he'd been shooting the breeze with a family down the road. "Sorry, guys," he'd shout to the parishioners as he threw on a chasuble and charged up the aisle. In addition to presiding at Mass on Sunday mornings, Costello ran a garbage truck that picked up trash from local cottagers. It was a way of bringing extra money into the church.

The silver-mining town was a perfect setting for Costello's reckless energy. The parish, the oldest English-speaking congregation in the diocese, had been founded in the early days of the silver-mining rush. Over the years, the ramshackle streets with their false-front store facings had seen their share of hard times and heartache. Long gone was the town's extensive streetcar system, live theatres and pro hockey team. (At the height of the silver rush, Cobalt and neighbouring Haileybury each had teams in the National Hockey Association. The Haileybury team was sold in 1910 to form the basis of the Montreal Canadiens. The Cobalt team folded a year later.) Now in the long shadow of decline, Cobalt survived on small mining operations picking the last bones from the depleted ore bodies.

But the working-class families of Cobalt's neighbourhoods – "Swamp Street," "Frenchtown" and "Pig Town" – retained the stubborn pride of a grander past. Through a rich oral tradition, locals championed the stories of heroes, outcasts and remittance men. Les Costello was already a legend by the time he arrived at St. Pat's. Forty years later, his stories are still being told.

> *There was a family that lived in a shack down in Frenchtown. There was a mother with about ten kids. The dad was long gone and she lived a tough life. Father Costello watched out for all those kids. He was always making sure they were okay.*
>
> —*Cobalt story*

> *"He wasn't a hypocrite. He didn't hide nothing from you. If he wanted to have a beer he had it. If he wanted a second he had that, too. Did he swear? Sure. But I think that's what people loved about him. He was a human being just like you and me."*
>
> —*Len Bilodeau*

Les Costello's personality was heavily influenced by the hardrock mining culture into which he had been born. His entire ministry was spent in the mining towns. The unforgiving nature of the work, coupled with the barely tamed frontier geography and the multi-ethnic culture, moulded a distinct identity. "We live hard and party hard" is the coarse articulation of what the locals call "spirit." Mining culture has always valued the direct and immediate response as the most honest one – whether in partying, fighting or helping one's neighbour. This culture helped form the spirituality of Les Costello. No bullshit. Delivering the gospel straight – with no flowery chasers.

"He used to drive up to the house at night," recalls Len Bilodeau. "He'd say, 'Get your coat on, we've got a job to do,' and off we'd go to help some family."

Costello's insistence on treating the works of mercy as a team sport where everyone got "ice time" was founded in the fundamental Catholic belief that salvation is not simply a personal experience but is linked to a much wider communal responsibility.

"We must be saved together," wrote French writer Charles Péguy. "Together we must all return to our Father's house. What would God say to us if some of us came to Him without the others?"

Costello brought people with him by treating the work as a grand adventure. Meagre indeed would be an outing with Costello that wasn't worth at least one good laugh to tell about afterwards.

"One time we went to Merv Lavigne's house to move some furniture that was down in the basement," recalls Len Bilodeau. "We got down there and found Merv's golf clubs. Costello said, 'Let's practise.' We took the clubs out and starting swinging. No sooner had we started than 'poof!' a light smashed. Someone shouted down, 'Hey, what happened?' 'Oh, nothing,' Costello replied. We put the golf clubs back and then left with the furniture."

Timmins resident Gerald McNulty recalls inviting Costello over to pick up furniture for the poor. "The driveway was far from the house and the stove was heavy. A man of action, he then jumped into the truck, drove over the neighbour's lawn and over our lawn and parked right in front of the stairs. The men picked up the stove and put it in the truck. Father Les talked to me for a few moments and then drove away over the lawns."

People around Cobalt still tell stories about Costello's penchant for trying to con friends and parishioners into going "sharesies" on a used pickup truck. Anyone who made such a deal soon found out that sharing a truck with Costello meant having to share the work of loading used furniture.

The work was offset by lots of laughs and some serious life lessons. Frank Quinn recalls one incident in Timmins that left a lifelong impression on him. One night, fifteen-year-old Frank Quinn was hitchhiking home from a hockey game when Costello pulled up in a car.

"I need some help delivering groceries and there might be trouble," Costello told him.

They drove up to a home where a family was living in very desperate conditions. Costello told Frank to wait by the car while he checked out the situation.

"You stay out here with the groceries. When I holler, you bring the boxes of food inside."

Quinn remembers seeing a woman with two young children in pajamas standing at the door. A very big man came to the entrance just as Costello rushed into the house. The sounds of struggle and shouting could be heard from the street. Finally Costello yelled out to Quinn to bring in the groceries.

"I came in and he had this man by the throat," recalls Quinn. "This guy was a big man but Costello was so strong."

Costello had the man pressed against the wall. Over the man's shouting, Costello was saying, "Listen, you doughhead. If you don't want to take this, at least let your kids eat."

As the man continued to struggle, Costello steadily talked him down. Knowing the man's pride was deeply wounded by his inability to feed his own family, Costello spoke of this charity as a kind of loan from one man to another. "You'll be able to get a job," he was telling him. "You'll get back on your feet. You can pay me back then."

Frank was shocked to see the anger melt away and the big man fall on his knees in front of Costello, crying.

"I'll tell you," Frank says, "That image left a lasting impression on me. I really think Cossie was a bit of a miracle worker."

"People talk about his language, but he was very concerned about using words that offended God. I used to always say the J.C. word and it would make him very cross. 'Listen,' he'd say, 'if you gotta release steam, just say fuck. It may offend people but it doesn't offend God.'"

—Frank Quinn

"Miracle worker" wasn't the term used by some who heard Costello speak at regional gatherings of various Catholic faith organizations. Costello was notorious for his use of foul language and locker-room humour at these events.

Margo (Quinn) Young says that his crude humour offended a number of people.

"There were people who didn't like him. They didn't like the crudeness. They didn't think it should be part of a priest. But it was the same with people from any denominational background. There were those who didn't like what he was and those who did. I didn't like the crudeness but after awhile, you learned to look beyond it and see the whole man."

"I think some of the older folks disapproved of him," recalls Len Bilodeau. "Some of his jokes were pretty raw but the younger crowd found him very funny."

Bilodeau believes the jokes were an integral part of Costello's grassroots theology.

"He believed in laughter. You were relaxed with him at church. You wanted to pay attention because you didn't want to miss anything he might say to somebody."

There are those who have suggested that Costello's rough humour was a front to hide his own insecure self. Others say Costello was simply playing for the blue-collar crowd. After all, there has been no shortage of clerics who have tried to develop a street credibility by adopting a rough-talking persona. But false bravado would have worn thin very quickly among the people of the mining towns.

Costello's almost brazen disregard for the sanctimonious drew a protective and deeply empathic response from the working-class congregations in which he served. They saw him as one of them because he made no distinction between the pious or the card-playing crowd.

But Costello's lack of distance with his parishioners was creating a headache for the new bishop, Jacques Landriault. Stories of Costello's involvement in drinking and card parties were filtering up to the diocese office in Timmins. In 1973, Landriault decided it was time to clip Costello's wings. He was moved out of Cobalt and back to Nativity parish in Timmins, where he was placed as third in command under his venerable old friend Canon Jones. If Costello was taken aback by this demotion, he didn't show it.

"Les had a strong sense of obedience," says Father Des O'Connor, who worked with him at Nativity. "If the bishop called him in, he'd tell the bishop exactly what he thought, but he'd say, 'If you want me to go, I'll go.'"

George Stefanic puts it this way: "If the bishop said jump three feet, he'd either jump ten or not at all."

Landriault had demoted Costello as a way of trying to rein him in, but it didn't seem to have much influence. Costello was back on his home turf and carrying on as he had before. One parishioner explains, "At Nativity, Costello was seen as not representing what a priest should have been. He'd be out partying until three or four in the morning."

D'Arcy Quinn recalls the Nativity parishioners' initial culture shock at his arrival. "The older people really frowned on him when he first came. But soon after he had a packed house on the weekends."

12. A Priest and the Sacraments

This bishop met this priest who lived in a really isolated community. The bishop asked him how he was coping with the isolation.

"Oh, I do fine," the priest replied, "as long as I have my Rosary and my margaritas."

The bishop came to visit him one time. "Would you like a margarita?" the priest asked.

"Yes, I would," replied the bishop.

"Hey, Rosary," yelled the priest, "get the bishop a margarita."

—Father Costello pulpit joke

Throughout the winter there was a steady game of pickup hockey on the outdoor rink at the bottom of the hill on Spruce Street in Timmins. Every day, nineteen-year-old Dan Bagley watched the local guys play shinny as he walked to work at the CFCL television station. Bagley was from a big Irish clan in Toronto (the Mulvihills) and it was his first time away from home. He was a stranger in this town, isolated and lonely. He was also convinced that he had landed a job in what he called the "A-Hole" of creation. One day he stopped at the rink with his skates and asked if he could join in the play. A former St. Mike's student, Bagley considered himself a pretty good hockey player.

Sticks were tossed in the centre of the rink and the lineup of the teams was drawn. Just then, a grizzled man with a big toque and a ripped coat came down the hill with his skates. Bagley had no idea who the guy was. The stranger was picked for the opposing team and Bagley found himself facing off against him.

"We were playing against each other like it was the Stanley Cup," recalls Bagley. The game ended when Bagley took a stick in the face and ended up with seven stitches. The next day, the same man came storming into the television station where Bagley was working. "Hey, Coles," he shouted up the stairs to the station manager, Terry Coles. "You got a little prick working for you and I want him for a Flying Fathers game."

Coles told Bagley to get his skates and get going. This was Dan Bagley's first introduction to Father Les Costello and the Flying Fathers.

Costello drove Bagley down to Manitoulin Island, where the Flying Fathers were playing a game against a local Ojibway team. Costello had snagged Bagley because he was seriously shorthanded – having only managed to put together a line of seven players and a goalie. As Bagley stepped out on the ice, Costello told him not to take the game too seriously as it was all in fun. On that first shift a big Native player came skating over and knocked Bagley out. As Bagley was hustled back onto the bench, Costello jumped on the ice and knocked the guy flat. As the man tried to get up, another priest made sure he went down for the second time.

"These are my kind of guys," Bagley thought. Soon after that first game, Costello showed up at Bagley's place and said, "We got a job to do." The "job" was moving a massive refrigerator up the narrow stairs to what Bagley remembers was "a real dive."

Inside they met a woman and four children. As Bagley and Costello struggled with the fridge, the woman sat at the table crying.

"What the hell's the matter with you?" Costello said in his gruff tone.

She said her husband had left her and she had no money for the rent. She needed $300. Costello reached into his pocket and threw $410 on the table.

"There's $300 for the rent," Costello said. "You got $110 left for the kids and you're better off without that bastard."

Bagley was hooked. He became Costello's inseparable sidekick – working with the poor and playing with the Flying Fathers. For a number of years he was the only non-priest on the Fathers' touring lineup. During one tour of the Yukon, a reporter asked Bagley if, as the only lay member of the team, he was considering entering the seminary. Bagley shocked himself by blurting out that he was indeed thinking of becoming a priest.

"What the fuck was I saying?" Bagley later confided to Costello as he tried to articulate his own confusion about his role with the Flying Fathers.

"Hey, Bagger," Costello responded, "maybe God is calling you."

In 1979, Bagley entered the seminary, having been deeply influenced in his vocation by his friendship with Costello. Following his ordination he returned north to work alongside his best friend and mentor.

Father Costello was the guest speaker at a Bobby Orr celebration in Parry Sound. The event was held at the local Orange Hall. It was a really hot day and everyone was sweating.

Costello stood up and said, "If there's Orangemen here today, I just want to point out that if you think it's hot now – wait until judgment day."

—Father Costello story

Costello maintained a public persona as a raunchy, tough-guy priest. It helped divert attention from the deep sensitivity he was able to convey when dealing with people in pain. One of the areas where his ministry was most noticeable was his work with the sick and dying. Florence Kelly, a pastoral care worker at St. Mary's hospital in Timmins, developed a deep bond with Costello through his hospital ministry.

"All the priests signed a register when they came in to administer the sacrament at the hospital. But not Les. He didn't believe in rules. You could always tell that he'd been in the hospital because any patients he'd visited had a St. Martin de Porres medal."

One time, Kelly called Costello to come administer the last rites. An elderly man was close to dying. Finally, the silence of this tense vigil was broken by the sounds of loud, off-key singing coming from down the hall. Costello stepped into the hospital room decked out in a toque, big rubber boots and a red plaid hunting jacket full of holes.

He went over to the bed, took a look at the man and exclaimed, "Holy shit, you look like you're dying!"

It may have seemed like the most inappropriate introduction one could make in such circumstances, but even the old man had to laugh. The joke eased the tension in the room. The priest then began to administer the sacrament of the sick. By the time Father Costello was ready to leave, the old man was beaming.

"Look at you. You're not ready to die," Costello stated. And he was right. The man lived.

Kelly says Costello's loud singing in the hallways was offset by the care he showed at the bedside. One time, after anointing an unconscious patient, he stood at the end of the bed staring intently at the man.

Florence Kelly was unnerved by Costello's determined silence. Not knowing whether he was praying or not, she spoke up. "What are you doing, Father?"

"Never mind," he said brushing her question aside.

When Costello snapped out of this mood of concentration he turned to her and said, "He'll be up and eating by lunch."

Kelly just shook her head in disbelief. It was impossible that this patient would recover so quickly. When lunch came around she went back to the man's room and, just as Father Les had predicted, he was sitting up in bed eating.

Florence Kelly came to rely on Father Les's uncanny sense for knowing who would live and who would not. After anointing one woman he said simply, "That's it, Flo, she's going." Soon after, the woman died.

"You couldn't have this sense about whether people would live or die without having a very deep spiritual life," Florence Kelly says. "He kept this spirituality very private, but he seemed to be able to influence people that other clergy were unable to reach."

Kelly says she could count on Costello to come to the hospital at any time of the day or night. It made no difference to Costello whether the patient was a parishioner, a lapsed Catholic or a non-Catholic.

Many non-Catholics and agnostics called on Costello when they found out they were suffering from terminal illnesses. Costello didn't quibble with the church-going or denominational status of the families who came looking for help.

"He was the priest for people who didn't go to church or who weren't Catholic," recalls Margo (Quinn) Young. "He would go into the hospital to bless people who had no church background. He regularly did church funerals for Protestant families."

Costello established a reputation as the priest for non-churchgoers. George Stefanic, a long-time parishioner at St. Alphonsus, explains: "The way of the traditional priest was that if you were not a Catholic you would never be buried in the Church. Father Les deviated from this norm. He would never let anyone go to his grave without a burial in the Church. Any derelict was given a proper burial. A lot of non-Catholics asked Father Les to handle their funeral. He'd say, 'What's wrong with giving them a funeral? We're all going to the same place.' He was a man for everybody."

Gord Lapierre, who came to know Costello at Nativity parish in Timmins, provides this story: "When my uncle died, none of the churches would do the funeral because the man wasn't a churchgoer. Les said, 'Sure, I'll do the funeral. This man worked hard in the mines all his life. He deserves a funeral.'"

While the post–Vatican II Church has officially claimed support for ecumenism, it has remained very rigid about priests conducting church services for non-Catholics. Costello's actions certainly skirted church rules, but he was well within the spirit of his patron St. Martin who, when confronted by church superiors about breaking rules in his service of the poor, replied: "Forgive my error, and please instruct me, for I did not know that the precept of obedience took precedence over that of charity."

Costello's position was also supported by the ancient church obligation to practise the spiritual and corporal works of mercy. Providing a proper burial is one of the seven corporal works of mercy (the others are feeding the hungry, giving drink to the thirsty, clothing the naked, giving shelter to the homeless, visiting the sick and freeing the prisoners). The obligation of Christians to practise the works of mercy is derived from chapter 25 of Matthew's gospel, where Jesus makes it clear that not only salvation, but the presence of God, is to be found in the service of the marginalized:

> Come, you who are blessed by my Father; take your inheritance, the kingdom prepared for you since the creation of the world. For I was hungry and you gave me something to eat, I was thirsty and you gave me something to drink, I was a stranger and you invited me in, I needed clothes and you clothed me, I was sick and you looked after me, I was in prison and you came to visit me...

Costello's approach to funerals was a blend of his deep love of the sacramental nature of life tempered with Irish wit and irreverence. Gord Lapierre was present at a funeral where one of the pallbearers tripped just before the grave.

"Whoa," shouted Costello. "Stay out of the hole, that belongs to Izzie [the dead man]!"

Tim Miner remembers attending one funeral with Costello. "There were a dozen of us at the graveside. Les gave a very short service, and shortly after had everyone in stitches, recounting some of the adventures of my friend who had quite a misspent youth."

Costello then regaled the crowd with tales of one of his own siblings who once "borrowed" a fire truck and ran the siren blazing in the main intersection of South Porcupine.

Costello's relationship to his parishioners was very much defined by the way he administered the sacraments. He treated these sacred signs as occasions of joy. He wanted his families to see these mystical symbols as part of the natural fabric of their lives. In the Catholic faith the sacraments (baptism, eucharist, confirmation, reconciliation, holy orders [ordination to the priesthood], marriage, anointing of the sick) provide the framework for a life's journey in faith. These are not mere symbols but actual vehicles for bringing grace into our lives. Like the seasons in the church year, the sacraments mark the seasons of life. An active parish priest is present for all the important landmarks in a family's life.

St. Alphonsus parishioner Kate Jacksic provides this memory of Costello's relationship to her family through the sacraments: "Father Les was a very special friend to our daughter Brenda, who is developmentally challenged and non-communicative. She would attend Mass on Saturday evenings during her monthly visits home…. I asked Father Les if our Brenda could be confirmed even though she is unable to take Holy Communion. He said, 'Why not?' At the end of the service he put his arm around her shoulders and led her down the aisle singing 'For She's a Jolly Good Fellow.' We will always be grateful for his understanding and accommodating manner."

This accommodating manner was present when he taught children how to make their first confession. He used to sit in the confessional box and then pretend he couldn't get out. With his foot firmly pressed against the bottom of the door he'd pull on the handle and shout for help. The children roared with laughter as the door finally pulled inwards and Costello fell back pretending he had banged his head. To the children he was always known as Father Marshmallow.

Nervous grooms waiting to be married were often treated with a shot of rye in the rectory and a reassuring slap on the back. At one wedding he began the service by reading from the prayer book, "We would like to extend our deepest sympathies to the family of—." Throwing down the book he shouted over to the altar boy, "You gave me the funeral book. Go get the wedding book."

Costello's approach was very much a part of the greater notion of the sacramental nature of life being articulated in the post–Vatican II Church. The laity had become more involved in the sacraments and were encouraged to recognize the relevance of these ancient rites in the modern world. A pioneer in this approach was television host Bishop Fulton Sheen. Sheen's comfort with the television medium and his casual American presentation style served as the confident new face of the post-war Catholic community. In his book *These Are the Sacraments,* Sheen provides this interpretation of the sacramental nature of faith:

> No one can ever understand the sacraments unless he has what might be called a "divine sense of humor." A person is said to have a sense of humor if he can "see through" things; one lacks a sense of humor if he cannot "see through" things. No one has ever laughed at a pun who did not see in the one word a twofold meaning. To materialists this world is opaque like a curtain; nothing can be seen through it. A mountain is just a mountain, a sunset just a sunset; but to poets, artists, and saints, the world is transparent like a window pane – it tells of something beyond; for example, a mountain tells of the Power of God, the sunset of His Beauty, and the snowflake of His Purity.

Costello tried to make the sacraments accessible. It was his way of sanctifying the often hard lives of his parishioners. Needless to say, many young couples came to Costello hoping that the genial cleric would give them a quick blessing. No such luck. He was more than willing to turn down a couple if he felt that an underlying love and maturity of relationship was not present.

Father Des O'Connor explains: "He expected people to be true to their commitments – whether in marriage, the priesthood or the single life. Husbands had to be good husbands and fathers. Women had to be good mothers and wives."

When counselling couples who were on the verge of separation or divorce, Costello would immediately cut to the heart of the matter. "Do you love him?" "Do you love her?" If the answer was no, Costello would send them on their way. Without love there was nothing a priest could do to hold this union together.

When counselling one couple, Costello sized up the situation and led off with a slapshot – "Okay, who's screwing around on who?"

"He didn't believe in beating around the bush," says Bagley. "If there was a problem it had to be named and you had to take ownership of it."

Costello responded to families in crisis by trying, wherever possible, to support the role of the wife or mother. "The woman keeps the family together," he used to say, obviously influenced by the strong matriarchal presence of his own Irish upbringing. Costello was present for many mothers living in crisis situations.

Irene Friday, a mother of three who was widowed in 1972, recalls Father Les watching out for her teenage children and coming by on the weekend to play cards. He'd always bring over people for Irene to meet. "He said I needed to have some fun."

Costello always led the night off with a prayer – "St. Ann, St. Ann, send Irene a man." (Friday says Costello's prayers were unsuccessful.)

Another woman who was having a difficult time with her husband remembers Costello coming by to drink tea and watch the hockey game with her family. "I was having marital troubles but he always made them go away."

To a young woman who was leaving a bad relationship, Costello brought furniture and food for her new place. He also brought a new frying pan. "Hit him with this," Costello suggested.

"I met him in 1973 when he came back to Timmins. I'd never seen him before. I didn't know who he was. We were playing old-timer hockey and got into a roughing match. Both of us were thrown in the penalty box.

While we were in the penalty box I heard someone call him 'Father.' I said to the guy, 'If that's your father you better teach him to act right.'

The guy responded, 'He's a priest.'

I said, 'Like hell he's a priest, after the kind of language he used on me.'"

—*Gord Lapierre*

"Les and Dan Bagley used to come by the house at any time of the day or night and jump in our pool."

—*Colleen Landers*

Costello offset his work as a priest by maintaining a very athletic schedule. He biked and played tennis in the summer. In the winter he skied and played hockey. When he wasn't on the road with the Flying Fathers, Costello played on a local old-timers hockey team. The league was strictly non-contact and Costello earned a year's suspension for his brand of tough body play. Not to be put off, Costello returned the next year and worked to keep his physical side under the radar screen of the refs.

In 1978, the old-timers team went to Copenhagen for a big hockey tournament. It was Costello's fourth hockey tour of Europe and his first without the Flying Fathers. Bill Cochrane, who was on the tour, remembers that the crowds in Denmark were anxious to meet the famous Flying Father.

The team was an assortment of local working guys. Nearly 30 teams from Canada and the U.S. came to compete against teams from Denmark, Switzerland, Norway and Finland. Mike Landers, who was on the Timmins team, recalls the Canadians' surprise when they realized that the European "old-timers" were younger and often from more illustrious hockey backgrounds.

"We got over there and found that the European old-timers only had to be 30 to play, whereas we had to be at least 35. The Finn and

Swiss teams were all ex-Olympians. We thought we'd be playing against guys like us who just played shinny."

Nonetheless, the Timmins team beat Finland 6-0 and went on to win a silver medal in the C division of play. Fifty-year-old Les Costello was named to the tournament's all-star team.

It was one more honour in what had turned out to be a long and oddly illustrious hockey career. But Costello didn't care too much about the honours of the game.

He came for the sightseeing and the camaraderie, and was always ready with his battle cry from local shinny games – "Win or lose, hit the booze!"

But Costello's carefree love of the game and life was about to undergo its toughest test yet.

13. St. Martin of Schumacher

"When news broke out that Father Les Costello was to be assigned as pastor at St. Alphonsus church, there was great jubilation among the people of Schumacher. I will always remember the first Sunday that he began his ministry in Schumacher. The church was filled to capacity and the liturgical celebration was one of great joy and hope."

—*Karen Stefanic, St. Alphonsus parishioner*

"He was never properly dressed for the bush. Anything you gave him he just gave away. He'd go out hunting in his shoes."

—*Colleen Landers, Nativity parishioner*

The streets are empty, people still hibernating under the inky black of an early morning winter sky. The only movement through the downtown streets of Schumacher is a steady stream of high beams cutting the ice fog. They turn at the intersection heading up the McIntyre Road for morning shift at the mine. But one car breaks out of the cavalcade and pulls off into the empty parking lot of the McIntyre Arena. Father Les Costello hobbles out with a cane in one hand and a pair of skates in the other.

He comes here every morning long before the arena opens. He comes in the darkness, free from the gawking eyes of the townsfolk. Like a broken-winged swan flapping futilely along the waters of the pond, he struggles along the boards. He's trying to force, through sweat and determination, a skill that once came effortlessly.

The doctors have told him he'll never skate again. Without toes a man has no centre of balance. Without toes a man loses the power of propulsion. But every morning Costello pushes himself out from the boards to find his way on this expanse of ice, searching for that mysterious key that has been taken away.

It's not just about playing hockey. The football player can run or the swimmer swim, but only the skater knows what it means to fly. Any northern male might be awkward or cumbersome in shoes, but given blades and ice he gains the grace of a ballroom dancer. And so this damaged swan flaps along the surface of the Mac because he has no other choice. It's in his nature.

> *"He sought solace in the bush. He loved to fish for brook trout. After Mass we'd go down to Latour Creek. We'd stop at a bridge about four o'clock. He'd say, 'You fish here. I'm going further and we'll meet back here at eight o'clock.' Many times he scared me because he'd been gone so long that I thought he was lost. He'd just sit down somewhere out in the bush. He preferred to be alone out there."*
>
> *—Len Bilodeau*

Les Costello damaged his feet in a hunting accident in 1979. He had just taken charge of St. Alphonsus parish in Schumacher. The community had long been an enclave of Croatian immigrants, along with a smattering of Irish, Finn and Italian families. Schumacher was four parallel streets sitting on a winding ridge overlooking the McIntyre Mine complex. The main drag (First Avenue) consisted of the Croatian Hall, St. Alphonsus parish and a dozen or so beer parlours. George Stefanic, who was active on the parish council, remembers Costello's appearance at St. Alphonsus as the coming of a "whirlwind."

"When he came to Schumacher he was like a breath of fresh air but he caused a real commotion. Our people were used to a traditional, straitlaced priest. The first thing he did was take down all the old statues. These statues had been there for 30 or 40 years and the old-timers just went crazy."

To many of the elderly Slavic women, St. Alphonsus was like a link to the old country – it represented the tradition and stability of the Church. They didn't take well to the changes brought in by the upstart Irish priest.

"Will you take out the pews next so you can put in a hockey rink?" one woman demanded.

But if anything, Costello would have needed more pews in what, up until then, had been a very quiet diocesan backwater. Following his appointment, the congregation swelled with young families from the neighbouring parishes of Sacred Heart, Nativity and St. Joachim's.

"Father Les was a breath of fresh air for St. Alphonsus parish," confirms Diane Dwyer. "Sunday Mass was usually standing room only. Parking was scarce and you had to come early if you wanted your favourite pew. Father Les drew people to him and made everyone feel welcome in his church."

Costello had only been at St. Alphonsus for a few months when, in late fall 1979, he went on one of his usual hunting forays into the bush. He loved the solitude of the great northern forest. The only problem was that he was careless. Whether he was skiing, hunting or fishing, he was rarely dressed for the weather. He often headed off into the surrounding bush without telling anyone where he was going.

The forest of the Porcupine lived up to its namesake – the bushland jutted out across the back of the hardrock shield like the dense and impenetrable quills on a porcupine. Let the weather turn suddenly cold or the early winter light disappear from the horizon and the bush could swallow a man whole.

On this one day in late fall, Costello went out when the weather was already turning to freezing. He had arranged to meet a guide but got tired of waiting and decided to head out on his own. He shot a partridge and bagged it. His plan was to scout about for more birds and then head back to the rendezvous point. In the dense Jack pine muskeg, however, he soon lost his bearings.

Like all who realize they are lost, Costello initially thought it was simply a matter of following a straight line back to his starting point. But the line inevitably began to veer until he was moving around in a circle. And once the circle was complete, the options evaporated. His internal compass was gone. Whether he was five kilometres or 50 from his goal, it no longer mattered. He was utterly and totally lost.

The day wore on and the temperature continued to fall. Costello was now feeling the effects of being poorly dressed. Then, while trying to cross a beaver dam, he lost his balance and fell into the freezing water. As he tried to pull himself out, he lost his boot in the frigid muskeg.

He was now in deep trouble. His hands were freezing. His foot was exposed. Taking the still-warm partridge, he shoved it on his toes and then wrapped the bag around his foot. Darkness falls early at this time of the year and Costello realized that if his luck didn't soon turn he'd be dead. When the body of the partridge turned cold, Costello ate it raw to keep up his strength.

St. John of the Cross experienced his "dark night of the soul" in the austerity of a Spanish monastery. Costello experienced his dark night in the terrifying immensity of the frozen boreal darkness. As the situation deteriorated, he found himself exhausted, frightened and curled up against a tree. It was then that he mustered the strength to get on his knees and begin praying to St. Martin de Porres.

"St. Martin," he pleaded, "if you want me to do your work, you get me the hell out of here."

Meanwhile, back in town, word had gotten out that Costello was missing. People were in shock. George Stefanic remembers that many of Costello's biggest critics were overcome with grief.

"The people who had been most upset with him were literally sobbing in the streets when they heard he was missing. For these people, the priest was the centre of their lives. He replaced Christ walking on earth."

Dan Bagley was at the seminary when he got the word that Costello was lost. He went to the chapel and began a long, frightened vigil. Sitting in the chapel he wrote a letter to Costello telling "Cossie bear" how he had been an instrument of Christ in Bagley's life.

As Bagley was praying in the warmth of the chapel, Costello was praying amidst an increasingly deteriorating situation. It was then that he heard a distant gunshot from an Ontario Provincial Police search crew. Costello had just enough strength in his hands to fire off a return shot. The police found Costello with badly frostbitten hands and feet. He should have been flown out of the bush immediately by helicopter, but there was no landing access nearby. As well, his damaged limbs should have been kept cold until they could be slowly thawed out at a hospital, but with a gruelling thirteen-kilometre walk ahead of them, the police made the mistake of lighting a fire and allowed Costello to quickly warm his damaged appendages.

By the time he finally reached the hospital, he was in very bad shape. His hands and feet looked like they had been burned black. Father O'Connor remembers visiting him in the hospital. "Les never let you inside what he was feeling but I was surprised when he said, 'My toes are like ten terrible toothaches.' He was in real pain but he showed no outward sign of that pain."

Bagley also visited, bringing with him the letter he had written when his mentor was lost. Costello read it with tears in his eyes. Bagley had never seen him cry before. "Bagger," he said, "if giving my life would help you become a better priest, I'd let them take my life right now."

Costello didn't have to give his life, but his experience cost him seven toes. The doctors told him his hockey days were finished. His days of hauling furniture up and down the stairs appeared to be over as well, because he no longer had the balance for such activities.

He was determined that, crippled or not, he would come back and light a fire in the little town of Schumacher. He had made a promise to St. Martin on that cold night, and he was determined to keep his end of the bargain.

"When Costello was released from the hospital," recalls George Stefanic, "our whole church changed forever."

"Two Mormon missionaries had gone to the rectory to see Father Les. Later they came to my place. I asked one young missionary what he thought.

'This man doesn't dress like a priest. He doesn't act like a priest. His rectory's a mess. He really needs to get his act together.'

I said, 'Would you give me that shirt you're wearing right now?'

The missionary said, 'No, I need it.'

I said, 'Well, Father Les would give it to me if I asked, so don't talk about him – he's a holy man.'"

—*Florence Kelly*

Costello returned to Schumacher, seemingly the same outgoing, crude and funny man. He tried to cover up for the immense difficulty he had in walking and maintaining balance. He spent every morning at the McIntyre rink learning to skate again. He knew that if he was ever to get back on the road with his beloved Flying Fathers, he would need to find a way to offset the staggering physical debt he now carried with him. Despite the odds, he returned to the lineup a diminished but still exciting player to watch.

Those who were close to him noticed a subtler but no less dramatic change. Len Bilodeau recalls that Costello began avoiding the limelight – turning down media interviews and requests to speak at local banquets.

Among his fellow clergy, Costello came to be seen as a lone wolf. He stopped attending meetings with the diocesan clergy. He paid mere lip service to a number of the diocesan-mandated parish programs.

Shirley McGarry, a long-time member of the local Catholic Women's League, recalls Costello filling in random names on the committee sheets that had to be submitted to the diocese. The lists were intended to show the bishop that mandated programs were being implemented.

"He didn't try very hard to get the programs of the diocese up and running," one cleric remembers.

Although Costello never openly fell out with his fellow diocesan clergy, there were those who felt that he had unnecessarily cut himself off from their company. Father M.J. Scully was one who was frustrated by Costello's continual no-shows at clergy meetings. After one meeting that Costello had skipped out on, Scully drove over to the rectory to confront him.

"Okay, Skull," Costello said as he let Father Scully into the rectory. "What's up? Speak up. Get it off your chest."

Scully says Costello liked to dominate the conversation because it kept him from answering questions about himself and his motives. Despite the clash, however, Costello didn't want Scully leaving with hard feelings.

"It's okay, Skull," he said, referring to their arguing. "I just like to keep you bouncing on the ropes."

George Stefanic, who was superintendent of education of the local Catholic school board, says people were often frustrated by Costello's anarchic approach.

"Costello just wouldn't be tied down to anything. He didn't believe in any organizational methodologies. He just wanted to get the job done. But when you look at his record, he got people going to church. The finances were fine and the church was always well maintained. What was the more successful approach?"

Costello was very much a product of a generation of priests who saw the laity as taking orders from the priest. He had no intention of being constrained by an organized laity, any more than he would be constrained by the programs of the diocese. "He empowered the laity and yet never believed in any organizational thrust by the laity; he ran the church 'My Way,'" recalls Stefanic. "One time he called a couple of us together and said, 'Why don't you be the church council? Just don't bother holding any meetings.' We didn't meet for another 23 years."

14. The Face of Christ

"I made a Christmas tree every year for the church. I went home one night after leaving it in the porch of the rectory. I came back in the morning looking to finish it but it was gone. I asked him where it was and he said, 'Oh, a young girl was over last night and she was crying. She had nothing to give her kids for Christmas and no tree. I gave her the tree.'"

—Shirley McGarry

"I was sitting in the rectory one time with Frank Mahovlich, our friend Brian Grant and Cossie. There were appliances all over the driveway. There was a guy out there going through the appliances and Cossie looked out the window and said, 'Hey, get the fuck away from those appliances. I just gave you a stove last week. Get the fuck out of here.' He then went back to talking with us as if nothing happened."

—Pat Hannigan

The yard in front of the church looked like a perpetual lawn sale. The rectory was overrun with used clothes, food parcels and furniture. When the choir came in for practice it wasn't unusual to find a drunk sleeping behind the organ. The church basement had become a shelter for indigent people. The needs of the local poor were administered through the St. Martin de Porres Society – a parish-based volunteer organization set up by Costello. But in reality, people came because Costello welcomed them.

Costello's open-door policy disturbed many in the parish because of the chaos it was bringing into the church. One parishioner who had come over to unplug the clogged toilets in this burgeoning flophouse decided it was time to confront the pastor. He came into the kitchen where Costello was sitting eating lunch.

"Father," he pleaded, "why do you let these people sleep here? They dirty the walls, they plug up the toilets."

Father Les looked up from his sandwich. "Have you seen the face of Christ?" he asked.

The man said no.

"Well, neither have I," said Father Les. "And I don't plan on missing him when he comes."

To see the face of Christ has often been seen as part of a "higher" mystical journey of the saints. In serving the poor, the saint is not simply looking to alleviate suffering but is seeking the actual presence of God. As anyone who has worked with the poor quickly realizes, however, the "face of Christ" is easily obscured by the often painful and seemingly futile nature of the work. Humour, often absurdist humour, is a better antidote in such circumstances than overt piety. Costello's manic personality and dark Irish humour flourished in the chaotic atmosphere of the St. Martin de Porres Society.

One time a very drunk Native man came to Costello for money. Costello had given money to the man earlier and wasn't about to indulge him a second time.

The man grabbed hold of Costello and began shaking him. "This is my land you're on," he said.

"Well, if you don't get your hands off my body," Costello replied, "you're going to be lying out there on your land."

Another time, someone stole the television from the rectory. Costello stood up at the next Mass and said, "There's not much I want out of life.

I like to read and I like my TV. You can take anything else but I want that TV back."

The TV was returned.

Parish members regularly complained of the need to lock the church, but Costello didn't worry about break-ins or thefts. When the church microphones were stolen he simply walked down to the local pawn shop and said, "Those are mine." Nobody argued. The microphones were handed over.

Shirley McGarry remembers Costello giving his own clothes to people at the door.

"When people came looking for clothes, he'd say, 'Go upstairs. I think I have some sweaters in my drawer.' He'd give his own clothes away if people needed them."

Costello paid special attention to the struggles of young single mothers trying to hold their families together. "Save the family and you'll save the world" was his lifelong motto. Among those families he helped save were the children of Jerry and Sharon Twain, who were killed in a car accident in 1987. Their eldest daughter, Eileen, struggled with Children's Aid to keep her three younger siblings with her. The children often went to school with little more than mustard sandwiches for lunch. Father Costello went to bat for Eileen and did everything he could to keep the family from being broken up by Social Services.

Years later, when Eileen had changed her name to Shania and reached international stardom, she repaid Costello's kindness with the gift of a new organ for St. Alphonsus parish.

As George Stefanic says, "He would come across to people as very gruff, but personally he was very Christ-like. It's almost like he didn't want you to believe he was the way he was. He almost impersonated Jesus but he didn't want you to think that. He didn't want to be boxed in by your perception of him as a priest."

The parish was a community action centre. If the work outstripped volunteers, Costello wasn't afraid to wake neighbours up on a Saturday morning with a list of items to be delivered and families to be attended to. When Pete Babando first retired, Costello latched onto him because he owned a half-ton pickup truck.

"What are ya up to?" Costello would ask. "Can you go over to such-and-such a house and pick up some furniture?"

Once the furniture had been dropped off at the parish, Costello was ready with further orders.

Babando said he was doing so much driving he threatened to start charging mileage.

"You'll get paid in time," Costello said, pointing skyward.

Anyone with the misfortune of having a half-ton could count on Costello showing up with a long list of chores. Catholic or Protestant – nobody was safe from Costello's "volunteer army." Freddie Dwyer was a continual victim of Costello's habit of borrowing the pickup truck. One time Costello drove Dwyer's truck right through a red light and broadsided a police car. The officer came out limping.

"Oh, I'm sorry," Costello exclaimed. "Are you all right?"

"I'm limping because I just had a vasectomy," said the cop.

"Oh well," responded Costello. "It serves you right, then."

The community came together to put an end to Costello's borrowing. They bought him a brand-new $20,000 pickup truck. But Costello wasn't having any of it. Within a week the truck was gone and an old beat-up wreck was in its place.

When confronted by parishioners, Costello replied, "I didn't need that damned truck. A family in Timmins got burned out last week. I sold the truck and brought them furniture."

The poor state of Les Costello's pickup truck was something of a local joke.

"The truck would never have passed a mechanical," recalls Rick Young. "The police would turn a blind eye to him when they saw it."

Costello revelled in being in continual emergency response mode, but many volunteers found they couldn't keep pace. Mike Landers remembers days when Costello was the "first person I saw in the morning and the last person I saw at night."

Mike's wife, Colleen, became so frustrated at the way Costello was monopolizing her husband's time that she phoned the rectory and blasted him on the phone. "Do you want to be named in a divorce proceeding?" she said. "My husband is never home and I get call after call from all these single young women wanting him to come over and fix things at their apartments."

> *"I was newly separated with one child to look after by myself. There was no food in the fridge or pantry. Father Les had someone come by the house and deliver a few bags of groceries. He told the delivery person that I was bringing the food to someone else so I wouldn't be embarrassed."*
>
> —anonymous tribute left in the comments book
> at Costello's funeral

Costello's mission work could be interpreted as simply "on the fly" social work being conducted in a needlessly makeshift manner. A more organized response to local need might have proven more effective. After all, there was no shortage of wealthy donors who would have supplied the vehicles and dollars to develop an efficient structure for serving the poor. For example, after Costello's death in late 2002, Falconbridge Mine president Warren Holmes called the St. Martin de Porres Society to see if the group needed anything. "Yes," Rick Young replied. "We need another truck."

"Do you want $25,000?" asked Holmes.

"Oh no," replied Young. "Just an old truck."

Holmes made some calls in the local mining industry and the following day, Dome Mine sent over a 1997 4x4 in perfect condition. Such help would have been available to Costello anytime he asked.

Clearly, Costello's personality rebelled against the constraints of a more organized structure, but this resistance was also rooted in a grassroots vision of social action that was articulated by a number of twentieth-century Catholic organizations.

The Catholic lay response to "charity" had developed distinct forms of approach. The first was based on the professionally driven Catholic "charities" structure dealing with everything from crisis counselling to social housing. This format was very effective in mobilizing aid across a wide spectrum of Catholic parishes and community organizations. The other was the more "radical" grassroots approach, wherein the relationship between giver and receiver was considered more fundamental than the amount of aid being delivered.

Dorothy Day's Catholic Worker movement was the foremost advocate of this school of Catholic action. Her newspaper, *The Catholic Worker*, encouraged decentralized "houses of hospitality" across North America where idealistic Catholics (and non-Catholics) lived with the poor.

The Catholic Worker popularized Church teachings on social action. But its overall approach stemmed from a hybrid of nineteenth- and twentieth-century social action philosophers, from the anarchist Russian Prince Kropotkin to the French Catholic intellectual Emmanuel Mounier. Writing in the early 1930s, Mounier called for a new system of social change, "Personalism," that recognized the primacy of the person over the rigidity of Marxist or capitalist perspectives. *The Catholic Worker* reinterpreted Mounier's academic vision with street-level immediacy. In the soup kitchens of the inner cities, Catholics were invited to recognize the obligation of individual Christians to create relationships with the poor.

Costello was providing a similar experience to the people of the Porcupine region. The St. Martin's volunteers drew on a wide range of volunteers. One of the most difficult issues for these volunteers was to refrain from making judgments as they were drawn into the lives of dysfunctional families and individuals.

"Don't judge," he'd say. "You don't know the kind of family life they have."

Dan Bagley explains that Costello had good reason for drawing a hard line on those who felt the desire to be judgmental. "If we judged each other, we'd judge each other to hell. This is why we must leave the judging to God."

Dorothy Day, in one of her writings, described the dangers of judging the poor:

> Being judged is perhaps the greatest burden the destitute have to bear; the contempt, the judgment of others. There is always the assumption of superiority, of having in some way managed better, of knowing better, than anyone else, in the attitude of those who help the poor.... We intrude on them with our advice: "If you go to Mass each day. If you say your rosary; if you kept better hours; stopped drinking; chose some good work; built up in yourself a philosophy of work, of poverty." Oh yes, we have many plans to help the poor. If we could only feed them, shelter them without question, without assuming all the answers.

Costello could have certainly been more "effective" if he had adopted a more professional or bureaucratic approach. But he also understood that charity could be very humiliating to people on the receiving end. His deliberate lack of organized structure made it possible for the sobered-up alcoholic or the single mother to feel they, too, had a place in helping with Costello's work. He often offered to "trade" furniture and was always willing to accept "payment" in the form of gifts and crafts that he would then give to others.

The money that was continually being donated existed as a roll of bills in Costello's pocket. He gave the money out freely to parishioners, families and even waitresses.

Dan Bagley says that one time he and Costello were sitting in the rectory playing cards when they began to count up the resources spent in the previous month on the poor. Both agreed the total was $1300.

Just then a man knocked at the door. He said he had been helped by Father Costello when he was having a hard time financially in Cobalt. The man gave them an envelope and said it was his way of paying Costello back.

"Inside that envelope," Bagley recalls, "were thirteen $100 bills. Cossie and I both looked at each other and said, 'Holy shit.'"

Florence Kelly tells this story about Costello's loaves-and-fishes ministry:

> One Christmas Eve I was working on the manger and he came to me and said, "Flo, come sit here at my table."
>
> I said, "Father, I don't have time to sit at your table. It's Christmas Eve. I have family at home. I want to go home."
>
> He said, "Ah, shut up and sit at my table."
>
> I said, "All I have is ten minutes."
>
> He said, "Good, that's all I need."
>
> I sat at the table in the rectory; the hall was filled with wrapped boxes. The doorbell rang and Father Les told me to go answer the door. It was a person asking for food so I gave them a box.
>
> The doorbell rang again and I gave out a second box.
>
> The doorbell rang a third time and there was someone with a box to drop off.
>
> Father Les said, "Okay, time's up. You can go."
>
> I said, "Wait a minute. What did I miss here?"
>
> He replied, "I wanted you to see that I never run out of groceries here no matter how many I give out."

Costello gave the public impression of a man who was continually seeking out the heart of the action. And yet he carefully nurtured his hidden reflective side. At night he would retreat to his room to read works of history, politics and religion. Costello ploughed through books at a surprising rate.

He read the writings of Catholic dissident theologian Hans Küng. Küng, a former adviser to the Vatican Council, has long been a *persona non grata* in the Church for his questioning of Catholic authority. In a

May 2000 interview, Küng accused Pope John Paul II of "betraying" the spirit of the Vatican Council.

Costello was also a big fan of G.K. Chesterton, author of the classic Catholic defence *Orthodoxy*. Chesterton was both an erudite philosopher and an irreverent champion of the working-class culture of his time. His ease with language and piercing humour appealed to Costello on many levels. Typical of the Chesterton wit is this passage from his book *The Common Man*:

> There has appeared in our time a particular class of books and articles that I solemnly think may be called the silliest ever known among men…. On every book stall, in every magazine you may find works telling you how to succeed. They are books showing men how to succeed in everything…. These writers profess to tell the ordinary man how he may succeed in his trade or speculation…. There may be definite methods honest and dishonest that make people rich; the only instinct I know which does is that instinct that theological Christianity crudely describes as the 'sin of avarice'…what is at the bottom of these books and articles is not mere business; it is not even cynicism. It is mysticism; the horrible mysticism of money.

15. A World in Change

"One time I was talking to Les about what was going on in my life. He said, 'You know what your problem is? You have metal disease.'

'Metal disease? What's that?'

'You've got silver in your hair, gold in your teeth and lead up your arse. Get out and do something.'"

—Murray Costello

"He didn't talk about the crisis facing the Church, but you could tell he believed a lot of things would change for the better if the Church was willing to make these changes. He'd get up in the pulpit and he'd tell you what the bishop told him he had to say. But then he'd say, 'You have your own opinions. Vote with your heart and your head.'"

—Gord Lapierre

On hot July days, Costello could be seen riding his bike bare-chested through the streets of Schumacher. This is the way he went about his rounds of visiting the sick and the elderly. Coming up to Mrs. Dorothy McGarry's house, he'd pull out a ripped T-shirt from his carrying bag.

"I'd better put this on or old Dorothy'll give me shit," he'd say.

On hot Sunday mornings, he greeted parishioners without his shirt. He'd then throw on his chasuble when the time came to head up the aisle. When Ken Campbell, a journalist from the *Toronto Star,* came all the way to Schumacher to do a major profile on the famous priest, Costello told him to hit the road. Campbell wrote a story anyway, calling it "Father Les Won't Talk Hockey."

To the people of Schumacher, such behaviour didn't even raise an eyebrow. He wasn't a novelty. He wasn't a famous hockey-playing priest. He wasn't the priest of the poor. He was simply Father Les or Cossie. He was as much a part of the landscape of Schumacher as the broken pre-Cambrian rock jutting out along the sidewalks.

He spent summer mornings playing tennis with his best friend, Father Bagley. Following the game, the two would head back to the rectory for a glass of orange juice and a chance to read the local paper.

"You know, Bagger," Costello confided one morning, "if heaven's half as good as this, I'll be happy."

"Yes," Bagley agreed. "We've got the world by the tail."

In the winters, Costello was back on the road with the Flying Fathers. His damaged feet had cut down his ice time, but the crowds still came out in droves to see the famous priest. Unable to carry out the dramatic surges up the ice that had been his trademark, Costello assumed a role near the opposing goalie's net. The crowd loved it when the pass went to Costello and he put it in the net.

Like their limping team leader, the Flying Fathers were living on past glory. By the mid-1980s, it was becoming clear that the seminaries weren't putting out the same breed and number of priests that had sustained the Flying Fathers in their early years. The day was long gone when two or three young priests oversaw a local parish. The workload and isolation of these middle-aged priests was making it increasingly difficult for the team to recruit players who could commit to a 30-plus game season.

Father Bill Scanlan described the massive change affecting the Church in a *Toronto Star* interview in 1986: "Before the Vatican Council [ended] in 1965, we had all the answers. Afterwards we had no answers. Nearly all my friends left the Catholic Church."

The end of the road for the team was announced just after Costello's 60th birthday. Following a season in which they'd racked up 15,000 road miles and played eighteen games in 23 nights, the aging Fathers were calling it quits. The last game was scheduled for Copps Coliseum on February 28, 1988. Over 11,000 fans came out that night to watch Costello's squad of clowns. *Toronto Star* sportswriter Damien Cox stated that, with the demise of the team in the air, any hopes for a revival rested on the shoulders of 33-year-old Father Dan Bagley. Having already amassed fourteen years at Costello's side, Bagley just couldn't turn his old friend down.

"The Flying Fathers were ready to die," Bagley recalls, "but we kept it going because of our love for Cossie bear."

Bagley took over as captain of a reborn team. With a small band of young priests, including 29-year-old Father Murphy and Father Billy Brennan, he put the team back on the road for the 1989 season. Costello was right there with them.

The team was getting up to 300 requests for games a year. Costello managed to keep up his own priestly work and be part of the Flying Fathers by submitting himself to a punishing schedule.

Current team manger Frank Quinn explains: "One time we drove all the way from Timmins to Windsor (1300 kms) for two hockey games. We arrived late, then he got up in the morning, visited a hospital and a school, went over to Amhurstburg, played there and then drove home after the game so he could get to church. That trip wiped me out for a month but he'd say, 'You have to hold up your end of the bargain.'"

Bagley remembers driving all night through ice storms and blizzards to get back to their parishes. "We'd say the rosary as we drove," Bagley remembers. "Cossie loved the rosary and he would say it on all our drives. If he said he'd pray for you then he would pray for you. He would say your name as he prayed each prayer of the rosary. It didn't take long to fill up all 50 prayers."

As Costello continued to age, he refused to slow down. There simply wasn't enough time to do everything that needed to be done.

"He was a real speed demon," recalls D'Arcy Quinn. "He'd get mad if you didn't keep the speed up around 80 miles an hour. He'd tell you to pull over and let him drive. I used to tell him to read his book. As soon as he'd start to read he'd fall asleep and then I could slow down."

The cost to his health, however, had begun to show. In the early 1980s, he had his first heart attack. It was a minor "bump" that nearly bowled him over in the dressing room of an old-timers hockey game.

Mike Landers remembers going over to Costello when it happened.

"Are you okay? Something's wrong, Father."

"Nah, nah, nah," Costello waved him off. "Everything's fine."

A few years later he was hit by a much bigger "bump" and ended up being sent down to Toronto for triple bypass surgery. The new bishop of his diocese, Gilles Cazabon, ordered Costello to stay in Toronto until he was fully recovered. Cazabon knew that if Costello came back to Schumacher he would throw himself back into his work without taking the time to heal.

To keep up with the demands of the Flying Fathers, touring and team arrangements were taken over by laity. Frank Quinn, originally from Timmins, became the principal team organizer and manager. Rick Young, a stalwart with the St. Martin de Porres Society, took over as trainer. As the pool of available priests diminished, Costello turned to his lay friends to fill the ranks.

D'Arcy Quinn began touring with the Flying Fathers in the late 1980s. An employee at Kidd Creek Mine, his work schedule didn't permit him to be present for the 30-game schedule. Costello, however, thought nothing of phoning the manager of the mine and telling him in no uncertain terms that Quinn had to be given time off (with pay) because the Flying Fathers needed him.

Quinn says touring with the Flying Fathers had a profound effect on his life.

"I'd always played for the competition. I believed it was about trophies and accolades. With the Flying Fathers you couldn't wait to get the game over with so you could go out and meet the people."

On nights when the team wasn't playing, the priests set up discussions about faith, justice and world issues.

Margo (Quinn) Young says that as much as Costello liked to pretend the Flying Fathers were just wild boys on the road, the lay members of the Flying Fathers brought back a very different picture of him.

"My brothers went on the road with him a lot. They said, 'You think you know this man. You have no idea of what he is really like.' They saw how contemplative he was on the road."

"He was given a brand-new leather jacket at a Flying Fathers event. They came out of a restaurant and there was a homeless person shivering. Father Les gave him his jacket. Someone said, 'Les, what the hell are you doing?' He said, 'He needs it more than I do.'"

—George Stefanic

The Flying Fathers had been formed to inspire people with an example of an active and heroic priesthood. By the late 1970s, men who fit this description were starting to leave the priesthood or drop out of the seminaries. This first wave of the priest crisis began in the late 1960s as thousands of young priests left their vocation for the married life. The bleed-off continued throughout the 1970s and 1980s.

In 1990, Father Dan Bagley sat down with his best friends – his fellow Flying Fathers – to tell them that he, too, was leaving. Bagley had fallen in love with a woman. He was deeply conflicted over the choice he had to make.

"The priesthood is a very lonely life. People are always taking something from you. Somehow you have to find a way to restore what's been taken. Cossie-bear found his escape in sports. It was his escape from all the shit that would go down at the parish."

Bagley found his escape in love. Although he was deeply committed to the vocation, he was tired of the loneliness. He wanted a family. At age 36, Bagley knew only two skills – playing hockey and serving Mass. He left the priesthood with no savings to face the difficult road of building a secure life for his new family.

The loss of a priest like Bagley made it clearer to Costello that the Church was losing high-calibre priests because of its refusal to move beyond the limitations of a celibate priesthood.

"The first person through the door to support me after my decision to leave was Cossie. He told me that some men had more than one vocation. He told me that I'd be as good a priest married as unmarried."

The crisis in vocations depleted the Church of much of its young and vital blood. The second wave of the "crisis," however, was much more damaging. Throughout the late 1980s and 1990s, the Church was hit by one sexual abuse scandal after another. In Canada, the crisis first appeared with the revelations of abuse at the Mount Cashel orphanage in Newfoundland. In the United States, it appeared as a seemingly anomalous series of incidents in parishes in Louisiana.

Over the next decade, a persistent pattern of sexual abuse emerged across the North American Church. The seeming failure of Church officials to stem this crisis left an impression of a hierarchy intent on damage control or cover-up.

Front-line priests were left to deal with the guilt, suspicion and shame of these unrelenting revelations. It was a disheartening time to be wearing a Roman collar. Among the privacy of his close friends, Costello confided his fears and frustration about a church that was afraid to open the ranks of clergy to badly-needed new blood and energy.

"I think Father Costello realized the need to get the vocation opened up to more people," recalls D'Arcy Quinn. "He wanted women involved. He could see that the vocation was dwindling and wanted the energy that other people could bring into the priesthood."

Costello and Bagley spent a great deal of time talking about the fundamental systemic problem plaguing the Church in this era of crisis.

"The hierarchy is an old-boys network," says Bagley. "Costello used to say that the reason they don't allow women priests is that the women would do a better job and we'd be out of a job."

The need for the inspiring outreach work of the Flying Fathers was greater than ever. People needed positive role models of the clergy. They needed to have their confidence in the Church restored. Year after year the aging Costello pushed to keep the team active on the road. It was a team that was increasingly filled with lay friends and old hockey buddies. But to the crowds who came out, the legendary "Flying Fathers" were still a thing of magic. "The miracle continues," he used to say every time a tour began or ended.

I remember Father Les calling out before Mass asking, "Who's going to serve Mass? We need some altar boys."

My sisters and I just sat there as he tried to round up the boys. Then he noticed us and said, "All right, come on up, girls."

And so we served with such pride (although I was quite shy) and felt so good to be the first girls to serve Mass alongside our dear Father Costello.

—note left by the Buchar girls following Costello's funeral

Throughout his life, Costello maintained the piety of his boyhood faith. He loved the sacraments, the rosary and the adoration of the Blessed Sacrament – expressions of faith that had been nurtured in a culture of the traditional Catholic working-class family. But the fact was, by the 1980s, the pious culture of the North American Catholic working class had all but disappeared. Costello, like other priests in the north, struggled to minister to the changing lifestyles of his parishioners. But the priests were caught between the changed values of the laity and a Church that was becoming increasingly inflexible to the changing realities of North American families. This inflexibility had, ironically, begun the first year Costello was installed at St. Alphonsus. Throughout 1979 and 1980, then newly elected Pope John Paul II issued a series of directives that made it clear that the open dialogue of Vatican II was over.

The direction of the North American Church was illustrated in the 1980 gathering of U.S. bishops, which called on the Vatican to recognize the legitimacy of the laity's opposition to the Catholic Church's stance on contraception. Archbishop John Quinn of San Francisco pointed out that only 26 per cent of the clergy believed that artificial contraception was a sin.

Said Archbishop Quinn, "The widespread theoretical and practical opposition to the teaching on contraception constitutes a profound theological and pastoral problem for the Church."

The Canadian bishops echoed similar concerns. They called on the new pope to recognize the need for "greater flexibility" in dealing with remarried Catholics and with the desire of married couples to practise contraception. Reverend Joseph McNeil, president of the Canadian Conference of Catholic Bishops at the time, spoke of the "anguish and anger" that existed within the Catholic laity over the Church's positions on birth control, remarriage and divorce. He called on the pope to provide the Canadian Church with the ability to deal with such issues.

This "anguish and anger" was reflected in the fact that young Catholics, who a generation ago would have been active members of a parish, were giving up on the Church.

The bishops' hopes for a greater dialogue were quickly frustrated. Despite his enormous popularity with average Catholics, John Paul II moved the Church along a road that brooked little dissent or discussion. This hard-line tone was set during the Pope's first visit to North America in 1979, when he shocked the American Church by refusing to allow women to serve communion during his Masses. He then quickly moved to outlaw the very popular and common practice of general absolution, which had replaced the old-style confessional. Absolution was given at a special reconciliation Mass where the laity were absolved of their sins through either a private confession with the priest or as simply part of a general forgiveness for the congregation. Once general absolution was abolished, the numbers of practising Catholics who went to confession dropped dramatically. As well, he ordered the bishops to take a harder line on dealing with divorce and contraception.

Rome was determined to bring the laity back into line with the pre–Vatican II devotional church. Priests were told not to baptize children of families who were not practising Catholics. When young couples came home from university to get married they found themselves having to prove they had been active churchgoers while they were away. Costello, who was very much a product of the pre–Vatican II Church, recognized that Rome's intransigence was only serving to widen the gulf between the laity and the Church. For example, young couples that were refused marriage or whose children were refused baptism were unlikely to raise their children in the faith.

"If we keep making it hard for people, they just won't come back," Costello confided to parishioner Colleen Landers.

The hardest line taken by the Vatican was in dealing with divorced Catholics. The increasing numbers of divorced families lived a shadow existence in church communities. If they wanted their new marriages blessed, they would have to leave behind the faith that had nurtured them. Costello, the lone wolf, continued to welcome the divorced.

One parishioner explains, "He would say to me, 'If a previous marriage didn't work out and these people have a deep faith and want to come back to the Church, how can I keep them out? If they come to me, why would I turn them away?'"

Bagley says Costello's willingness to provide the sacraments to people whom the Church would otherwise reject was based on his belief that he was simply doing what Jesus would have done.

"Jesus always took people where they were at. If a marriage broke up, it broke up. Costello would say you have to treat people with dignity, make them feel good about themselves and welcome them back in so they can get on with their lives. If parents who weren't married came to have a child baptized, Costello would welcome them in. He believed that every child should be given the graces of the Church."

Another sign of Costello's willingness to step outside the strict rules being laid down in Rome was the fact that a number of Protestant families had become part of the life at St. Alphonsus. Billie Babando remembers Costello casually mentioning one time how many Protestants regularly took communion. The comment surprised her, because even in the tightly knit parish community she didn't know that some active members weren't Catholic.

"He served everyone. He said better they come here than they don't go at all."

Babando believes that Costello worked hard to protect the people at St. Alphonsus from the changes that were happening in the larger Church.

"People went to St. Alphonsus because they felt comfortable. There were no politics in that church. I think people who went to the church felt like he did. We all felt welcome. People felt comfortable. We liked one another."

In 1997, Costello celebrated his 40th year in the priesthood. The whole community celebrated the event. Visitors to the church were able to see the dramatic renovations Costello had undertaken at St. Alphonsus. Local Croatian artist Ed Spehar had repainted the parish in a series of stunning murals. In a move that tickled Costello, Spehar painted the faces of local hockey heroes Frank and Pete Mahovlich as the faces of the cherubim above the baptismal font.

Costello's 40th-anniversary Mass was celebrated by Bishop Gilles Cazabon. The bishop had been a good friend of the people of St. Alphonsus and was very supportive of Costello's ministry among the poor.

"Bishop Cazabon understood Les," explains Colleen Landers. "The bishop was a real 'people' person. He saw the good work that Les did with the poor."

That same year, Cazabon was replaced as bishop of the Timmins diocese by Paul Marchand.

After 40 years in the priesthood, Costello, the maverick individualist, had begun to change. He looked to his parishioners for help in carrying out church functions. One of the most noticeable changes was the recognition that a parish council run by an active laity was needed.

George Stefanic says, "I went to him and said, 'Coz, we need a parish council.' He said, 'Okay, go do it.' Costello attended a meeting or two and then after that he was always 'busy.' I'm glad we got it going because it really helped us when he died."

Another dramatic change was that, in Costello's last year of life, he did not give out communion – he turned this task over to lay ministers. He may have made this decision because he was growing increasingly worn out, but he brushed away any questions about the move by saying it was time the laity had a chance to do the job.

Costello presented himself as someone too full of piss and vinegar to ever be sidelined. But many in the community were growing concerned about him. His housekeeper, Toni, watched over his eating habits like a mother hawk. As well, Costello had a half-dozen den mothers out to feed him. On any given night he could be walking into Schumacher homes like Helen Berlingeri's with the familiar shout, "Helen, what's for dinner?"

They all told Costello that he had to slow down. They told him he had to start giving up some of the workload. But day after day the poor kept coming. Day after day the sick needed to be visited and the children needed to be instructed at the school. No other priests were coming along to fill his shoes so he kept on as he had always done.

Frank Quinn shares this comment Costello made one time when they were travelling:

> He said to me that he didn't think that Jesus would have found the cross too heavy to bear because he knew he had a mission – that was to remove the sins of the world. He believed that because Jesus knew what that mission was, it would make it easier to bear the pain.

16. Pulling the Goalie

"The world is a crueller place without him."

—*Diana Cattarello*

Father Les was now an old man. He was three months away from his 75th birthday – three months away from having to submit his mandatory resignation to Bishop Paul Marchand. What then? During a visit with his old friend Dan Bagley, Costello blurted out his fears. "Bagger, what am I going to do? I've no pension. Where am I going to go?"

Under diocesan rules, all priests had to submit their resignation to the bishop at age 75. A retired priest received a monthly retirement supplement of $1,000 from the Church, plus the old-age pension from the federal government. In the best of all worlds, a retired Costello would have simply stayed on living at his beloved St. Alphonsus parish. But Costello knew full well that the future of his parish was in question. Already the bishop had started making major changes. In the southern part of the diocese, a number of parishes were being shut down or restructured. Word was that major changes in the English and French parishes in Timmins were in the works, and the future of St. Alphonsus was on the block. Before his final road trip, Costello confided in some parishioners that the parish was facing closure and the community would be moved. If St. Alphonsus was closed, Costello would be forced to ask himself some hard questions about where and how he was going to spend his final years.

As much as he tried not to show it, Costello was feeling the strain. Parish housekeeper Shirley McGarry recalls that in his final few months he was testy and sometimes short-tempered. "He was never like that before," she recalls. "Something was wrong."

Paramedic Gordie Lapierre noticed the change from the pews. "He'd been getting sick. I think he'd had a minor stroke. He was aging fast. Sometimes with the jokes he'd tell at Mass you could really take them either way. I'd just shake my head, wondering, because we had kids at church."

Costello was suffering from nosebleeds. He needed to rest. But then came the December 2002 road trip with the Flying Fathers.

His doctor told him not to go. Not that Costello shared this advice with anyone else. He was going because he had always gone. He was going because he needed to go.

The plan had been for Rick Young and D'Arcy Quinn to drive with him to the kickoff game in Guelph, scheduled for November 29. But D'Arcy had to cancel. His wife was undergoing cancer treatments. It was the first road trip in fifteen years that he missed. Costello really wanted Quinn with him on the trip. On the morning Costello was to leave, D'Arcy drove up. Costello was beaming. He thought D'Arcy had changed his mind. But Quinn had come to say goodbye.

The Flying Fathers played that Wednesday night in Guelph. Costello, as he always did, played the first two periods. He then showered and changed to meet the people when they came out in the lobby.

The team stayed over in Guelph until Saturday. Costello filled the time taking in movies – sometimes as many as four a day. It was a luxury he never had time for at home. The rest of the time he spent playing cribbage with his roommate, Rick Young. The games were played at five bucks a pop.

"We got up that Friday at seven in the morning and played crib until ten at night. We stopped for an hour and then each of us went for a walk."

After they'd ordered supper, Costello started writing some notes on a scrap of paper. He then fell asleep. (After his death, Margo [Quinn] Young received Costello's clothes and set out to wash them. Pulling out the piece of paper, she found it was a poem he was writing in tribute to her husband.) The team moved over to Kincardine on Saturday for an evening practice. Costello was out on the rink during the practice when he reached to kick an errant puck. Costello's balance, which had never been great since losing his toes, failed him and he fell backwards.

"When you fall like that, your neck isn't strong enough to hold your head and it just snaps back," explains Frank Quinn.

Costello was knocked out cold. An ambulance was called. He was mumbling and incoherent. After a few minutes he came to and was deeply embarrassed.

"Get me off the ice," he said.

As his teammates were helping him to the dressing room he kept telling them, "I'll be fine for tonight. I'll be playing tonight."

Quinn responded firmly, "Cossie, you're not playing anything."

Costello was taken to the hospital and released later in the day. He didn't want to go home. He didn't want anyone back in the Porcupine to know what had happened.

But Young phoned home to give the bad news anyway. Although people were worried, they assumed Costello would bounce back.

Costello went to the party after the Saturday night game and joined the team as they moved over to Peterborough. The team had three local games to play on the following Monday, Wednesday and Friday. But Costello was not recovering. He had broken some ribs in the fall and was suffering.

"He could get into bed," Rick Young recalls. "But he couldn't get out of bed. He was in great pain but he wouldn't complain."

On Friday morning, Young was getting worried. "Father, let's go to the hospital in the morning." To his surprise, Costello agreed.

Young got up the next morning at five for his regular walk. Costello called out to him and asked him where he was going.

Young said he was going for a walk. He asked Costello if he wanted to play their normal two games of early-morning crib.

Costello declined, saying he wanted to stay in bed. Costello had never turned down an early-morning game before.

Young returned at 7:30 a.m. and found Costello sitting in the chair with the comforter pulled up to his neck. The heater in the room was turned on full. Young made him a cup of coffee and the two began playing a game of crib. Costello spilled his coffee and was unable to move the pegs.

"You know, Father," Young told him, "you should shower and shave and we'll go to the hospital."

Costello went to the washroom but dropped his razor three times into the sink. At this point Young went to get help. While Father Pat Blake stayed with Costello, Young asked Father John McPherson to call an ambulance.

Costello was rushed to the hospital and began undergoing tests. The team members stayed by his side until it was time to leave for the game at 3 p.m. Young promised to return as soon as the game ended.

"As I said goodbye to him I saw tears in his eyes," recalls Young. "It was the first time I'd ever seen him cry. He was so tough. He never cried at anything. It was then that I realized that he was scared."

Dan Bagley arrived that night. Costello had now fallen into a coma. The former priest anointed Costello with the sacrament of the sick and placed his St. Martin medal on Costello's chest. At 10:45 that night, the Flying Fathers received the word that Costello was being rushed to St. Mike's Hospital in Toronto. They jumped into their cars and sped over to the hospital in Peterborough, arriving just as the air ambulance was leaving the ground. The story made national headlines. Back home in Schumacher, the community was in shock.

"There was sheer devastation in our community when we found out," recalls George Stefanic. "Man, oh man, it was awful. We prayed and prayed but we knew what was coming."

Monday, December 9, marked the birthday of St. Martin de Porres. The doctors made it clear to the family that if Costello recovered, he would be left physically and perhaps mentally incapacitated. Bagley stayed by him in the hospital throughout the day. After saying the rosary beside his bed, Bagley whispered in his ear, "Go to the light, Cossie. This is no life for you."

Costello died the following day. Looking back, Rita (Costello) Hogan says she takes comfort in the fact that her brother died before he had to submit his resignation to the bishop. "We'd ask him what he was going to do when he had to resign but he would never talk about it. The priesthood was his whole life. I think he was spared the choice."

The outpouring of grief overwhelmed the family. People treated his death like the death of a saint. The Costello family came north into a shocking whirlwind.

Like Les, the rest of the family was intensely private. They were not prepared for the public display of grief being exhibited in the region. In the newspapers, people were calling him a northern Mother Teresa. If he had been alive, Les Costello would have said it was a "horse's-ass" comparison.

The adulation and the grief were difficult for Costello's relatives to process.

"We were absolutely overwhelmed by the funeral," recalls Rita Hogan. "I remember going home that night and thinking, 'What is going on here?' People were making him into something that we didn't recognize. There were grown men crying all around us."

The family wanted a funeral in the parish. But with people coming from all across the north for the wake, it was clear that a parish funeral was out of the question. Shirley McGarry says the parishioners fought hard for the need to open the funeral up to as many people as possible.

"We knew that if the funeral was at the parish, a lot of the parishioners wouldn't be able to get in because it would be reserved for more important people. We wanted it at the arena because that's where he loved to be and everyone could be present."

In the end, the event was held at the McIntyre hockey arena. Over 2,000 people were in attendance.

The funeral began as a long march from the church to the arena. Among those walking were the Catholic Women's League, the OPP (Costello was the police chaplain), and the Knights of Columbus. They marched along the cold street as the church bell tolled.

Stefanic says there was an air of unreality about the event. "At the funeral I about expected him to jump out of the coffin and say, 'What are you doing, you dumb ass?'"

The funeral was attended by Costello's real congregation – Catholic, non-Catholic, believer, non-believer – people who felt very deeply that this man was *their* priest. At the end of the service, Costello's longest-serving teammates – his fellow priests – came up to the coffin and sang the old Latin prayer *Salve Regina*.

Then, as they moved to take the coffin from centre ice, something unforgettable happened. There was a momentary silence, as if people didn't know what to do. Was this really the moment when Les Costello would be heading off the ice forever? Spontaneously, people began to clap. The clapping echoed throughout the arena as people wept and cheered openly.

Father Des O'Connor remembers the sound of the cheering reverberating throughout the stands. "There was a real reverence in that arena. The participation was grand. I think the funeral really deepened people's faith."

Costello's funeral made all the national newspapers. The event was commented on by numerous national figures. Much was written about the irascible hockey-playing priest, but in the funeral book left at the wake, a number of anonymous tributes spoke of Costello's real legacy:

Thank you for dressing the prisoner at Monteith [jail].

I remember when he helped me when I lived on the street, he took me in when I needed a hand. And so I give him a hand when he needs it.

I was the town drunk and Father Les never refused me a meal or a place to sleep. Thank you, Father Les, for my fifteen years of sobriety and all the good things you have done for the less fortunate. May the Heavenly Father be with you now.

Costello was replaced at St. Alphonsus by Father Mitch Sliwa, a priest from Poland. Father Mitch was conservative but a dedicated parish priest. Attendance dropped off initially without Costello's warm and colourful style, but then it began to build back up.

Speaking in the months following Costello's death, Gordie Lapierre stated, "Father Les wanted to keep this church going. That's why so many people still go."

George Stefanic shared this view with a hope that under a new parish priest, the community would continue to grow.

"We are in a grieving process still. We have people at church who still expect Father Les to come out and punch them in the back as he used to do when he was going up the aisle. But our church is still full. It's like Father Les is still there."

Just as the parish struggled to continue, so did the Flying Fathers. With a winter tour booked along the east coast, Frank Quinn and Dennis Boyle, the two main organizers, worked hard to keep the team going. The team, like the parishioners, was moving forward, as much out of grief as out of a sense that Cossie wouldn't have allowed any time for backsliding.

Epilogue

L ess than a year after Costello died, St. Alphonsus parish received its second death notice. It happened during a regular Saturday evening Mass in October 2003. The pews were full, with a cross-section of ages and backgrounds. A choir of four local women sang in exquisite harmony. Rick Young was at the back of the church slapping his pals on the back as they came inside the doors. Pete Babando poked D'Arcy Quinn as he walked past him up the aisle – just the way Father Les would have done. The good-humoured spirit evaporated, however, as soon a member of the parish council stood up and read a terse message from the diocese. St. Alphonsus and Nativity parishes were being closed, and the congregations moved to a new English parish housed at the French Cathedral in Timmins. The woman concluded bluntly, "There's no point asking the parish council any questions. We don't know any more than you do."

People shook their heads and muttered. Some were visibly angry. An old Croatian woman started to cry. "Where am I going to go? Where am I going to go?" she said.

Rumours about the closing of St. Alphonsus had been swirling around the community for months. Bishop Marchand later told the media that he had made the decision after a great deal of reflection and concern. But on the streets of Schumacher, the move was like a hard kick on a tender wound.

"They would never have dared do this if Father Costello was alive," many said as they came out of Mass.

The parishioners filed out of the soon-to-be-closed church onto the newly renamed Father Costello Drive. D'Arcy Quinn noticed the irony.

"I think it's a pretty sad day when you rename First Avenue as Father Costello Drive and then close his church. We've already suffered enough with his passing. No sooner have we had to deal with his death than we are now faced with the closing of his church. It's going to put a big tear through this community."

Over the following year, the parishioners mounted a spirited defence of their parish. The struggle to save St. Alphonsus garnered national television and newspaper coverage. They even took their fight to Rome. But few expected the diocese or the Vatican to overrule the decision and protect this centre of Catholic faith and action. The closing of St. Alphonsus personified a new crisis in the Church. All across North America, parishes are being downsized, even in regions with an active laity. It's the response of a hierarchy that's simply run out of road. Faced with an aging priesthood and an unwillingness to appoint women, married men or an empowered laity to ministry, what other choice is there than to begin shutting down the parishes?

All of which brings us back to the cry of the old woman – where will these people go? The work of the Spirit must go on whether there are priests there to handle the work or not. George Stefanic believes that the fight for St. Alphonsus cuts right to the core of Les Costello's legacy.

"I sat on the diocesan committee that looked at these issues. We developed a rationale to talk to the bishop – What is a church? What is its function? What are the criteria for closing a church? The idea of the closing of the church is diametrically opposed to the experience of our parish. People are attending Mass here. Our church is strong. Father Les built a community. He did what Jesus would have done."

Among those who were closest to Costello, the death of their patron, followed by the closing of their parish, raised serious questions about the future of the outreach programs to the poor.

Rick Young explains, "I've dedicated part of my life to St. Martin's. It's very, very important to keep this work going. It'd make you cry to see some of the places you have to go into. I'm just hoping that somehow we can keep this organization going."

D'Arcy Quinn is hopeful. "He's got good, caring people in the church. I believe his divine intervention will make sure that this work survives."

Divine intervention? Does Quinn think Costello was a saint?

D'Arcy nods his head emphatically.

"To me he was a saint."

D'Arcy's brother, Frank, provides his own epithet: "If I ever had a hero it was Les Costello. He was the man."

While it remains to be seen how Costello's legacy will be remembered by the Church, his memory has been fittingly preserved by the people who loved him the most – the blue-collar families of the north. And what better tribute than to rename a hockey arena in his honour?

The Cobalt hockey arena is a typical northern cathedral of community spirit and memory. Youngsters tying up their skates can look up at an impressive lineage of hockey photos that date back to the legendary mining league teams of the early twentieth century. The arena's new centrepiece is a glass display case housing a statue of Costello, a commemorative Flying Fathers hockey sweater and numerous photos of the famous Stanley Cup–winning priest.

The official renaming of the Father Les Costello Memorial Arena took place on the August long weekend, 2003. A crowd of 500 people was on hand. Dignitaries, clergy and family members entertained the crowd with classic Costello anecdotes. A new sign was unveiled, inscribed with a typical piece of Costello doggerel: *"The wind may kiss the clear blue sky / the rose may kiss the butterfly / the morning dew may kiss the grass / and you my friend...I consider class."*

Following the speeches, a karaoke machine from the local Miner's Tavern was brought to the front of the makeshift open-air stage. All were then invited to join in a rousing rendition of Costello's favourite song, "The Wild Colonial Boy."

The sight of hundreds of people gathered outside a small-town arena singing an old rebel song may have seemed, at first glance, a rather odd way of remembering the man the papers dubbed "Northern Ontario's Mother Teresa." But the song certainly speaks to the spirit of Les Costello. "The Wild Colonial Boy" is, by its very nature, a group effort. It defies half-hearted or solemn renditions. After all, that's our lad James Duggan we're singing about. Sure he was a "terror to Australia," but he was also "his mother's pride and joy." And what family ceilidh hasn't raised the roof when the revellers hit the line "He robbed the rich and helped the poor"?

The large crowd that gathered on that dusty parking lot in a small town in northern Ontario sang along with greater joy than sadness. It was the Irish way. After all, they weren't simply paying tribute to a great hockey player or a man of God. They were celebrating the spirit of northern Ontario's very own wild colonial boy. And just like the legendary outlaw in song, it's likely that tales of Les Costello will continue to raise the roof at northern kitchen parties for years to come.

Notes

Introduction

The poem "The wind blew…" is the author's play on a poem written by Les Costello for his friend Len Bilodeau.

1. The Irish

The legends of the battles between the Shiners and the French workers are still told today in the Valley as "Big Joe Mufferaw" tales, Big Joe being the Anglicized name of the francophone fighting hero Joseph Montferrand. The story of the Shiners and Big Joe Mufferand is told in the book *The Lumberjacks*. I based some of the stories of the Ottawa Valley Irish on stories told by my own maternal grandmother, who was a descendant of the famine Irish who emigrated to the Ottawa Valley. Information on the square timber crews came from an interview I did for a CBC profile of David McLaren. His grandfather worked on the last White Pine flotilla to come out of Timiskaming. The migration of lumber crews north in the years following the square timber crews was based on timber licence records through the Gatineau, Kipewa and Timiskaming regions 1850–1874. This was work I carried out for the Algonquin Nation Secretariat in 2001.

2. A Child Is Born

The information on the Hollinger fire comes from newspaper records as well as the excellent account by Magne Stortroen in his book *An Immigrant's Journal*. Information on the ethnic make-up of the mining communities of the Porcupine was gathered during research for the book *Mirrors of Stone*. Information on the turnover rates among Canadian workers comes from the essay/lecture "Les ouvriers-mineurs de Timmins (1915–1940): Les canadiens-français, mais surtout les autres," by Guy Gaudreau. Information on the Irish connection to the English-speaking parishes of the Timmins diocese was pieced together through interviews conducted with Father

M.J. Scully and Father Des O'Connor. Information on Father John O'Gorman coming to Cobalt was gathered during the research for the book *We Lived a Life and Then Some.*

3. The Game

Much of the information was supplied through oral interviews. The information on Lou Gehrig came from a 1940 biography on Gehrig. Information on the mining hockey leagues was gathered through a number of years of research. Carlo Cattarello Sr., coach of the Holman Pluggers, provided a good oral record of the early sports years in South Porcupine. Gus Mortson provided information on the Kirkland Lake mining leagues for a CBC documentary profile I did on Mortson in 2000. Journalist Gregory Reynolds provided colour and context in his 2001 *HighGrader Magazine* article "The Rinkmen: Outdoor Rinks in the Porcupine," where he states that outdoor rinks in the 1940s were able to maintain ice from November to late April. Information on the early years of the NHL came from the book *50 Years of Hockey*. Information on Bickell, Smythe and the Coloured Line was gathered through a number of oral interviews.

4. A Church on Skates

Much of the information on these St. Mike's games is taken from Greg Drinnan's *History of the Memorial Cup*, reprinted in the St. Mike's 1998 publication "The Tradition Lives On." The Irish Catholic connection to Toronto hockey was noted in the name of its professional team, "The St. Patricks." Opinions of the school and its hockey emphasis differed among the various people I interviewed (other former St. Mike's students, not cited, also offered comment on the times). I tried to include the varying views and opinions on Conn Smythe. Information on the role of the Timmins diocese and hockey came from oral interviews with priests as well as perusing numerous newspaper microfiches over the last number of years. Details on the Holman Pluggers came through conversations with Carlo Cattarello Sr. and his son, Carlo Jr. Oral interviews provided the larger picture of the school and its times. Information on Barilko was gleaned from numerous family stories and the author's research.

5. Lord Stanley's Ring

The picture of the Leafs organization was filled out by the books *Images of Glory, 50 Years of Hockey,* the 1948 *Hockey Annual* and *The Death of Hockey*. Information on Costello's first goal of the 1948–49 season comes from author Kevin Shea. Conn Smythe's comments about violence in the game is from *The Death of Hockey*. Stats on Costello's years with the Leafs organization come from the official records. The story of Costello's relationship with the Leafs organization comes from oral interviews.

The story of Costello's decision to put the wrong name on the Stanley Cup came from Murray Costello.

6. The Summer of '50

The picture of life in the summer ball leagues was developed through a number of interviews, not necessarily connected with this project, including an interview I did with W.T. "Red" Phillips, former mascot with the McIntyre Mac Men in their glory days. The stories of Costello's ball-playing were related to me by a number of people. My uncle, Rodney Allen, loves to tell the story of Frank Chase tagging Costello at third base.

7. The Door Swings Both Ways

Details for this chapter were provided by Father Scully and Father O'Connor, both of whom were at St. Augustine's during the period Costello was there. I transcribed Costello's comments to a television reporter from a video of various footage of the Flying Fathers provided to me by Father John Caswell. No dates exist on the footage. Information on St. Martin de Porres comes from the religious pamphlets available at the back of St. Alphonsus church. I was indebted as well to Bernard Daly's excellent work, *Beyond Secrecy: The Untold Story of Canada and the Second Vatican Council.*

8. On the Mile of Gold

Information on the Vatican Council comes from a number of sources. The quote from Cardinal Roncalli is from the book *A Man Called John.* The story of Father Costello's prank on his mother comes from Anne Dmytruk. The story of Costello's desire to go on the missions comes from Father O'Connor. Information on the accident and death rates of the gold mines comes from work the author did over the last ten years, partly as a researcher for the United Steelworkers Union, and as an author. The claim that the average life expectancy of a gold miner was 41 years of age is based on a research project the author conducted in 1998 for the book *Mirrors of Stone.*

9. The Noranda Alouettes

Besides the oral interviews conducted for this book, I was aided by e-mail correspondence from Laura (Kruger) Landers and Tim Miner. The story of Father Caulfield answering the phone comes from the St. Alphonsus book of memories published after Costello's death. The story of Costello's showdown with his housekeeper comes from Dan Bagley. Information on Noranda Mines comes from numerous sources. See Mike Solski's book *Mine Mill.* The quote from St. Gertrude comes from Margaret Quigley's book *Dorothy Day: A Selection of Her Writings and Her Readings.*

10. The Flying Fathers

I am indebted to Father John Caswell, who provided video documentary footage and interviews with the Flying Fathers. Frank Orr's comment appeared in Jim Kernaghan's article "Flying Father really had wings on his feet," *London Free Press,* December 2002. Information on Father Bill Scanlan and Father Vaughan Quinn came from *Toronto Star* articles cited in the Bibliography. Other information came from various Flying Fathers' souvenir programs. Information on the priests and their development came from numerous interviews. The fact that some bishops did not want their priests to join the Flying Fathers came from an ex–Flying Father. Details on the Hollywood deal and Gretzky's screen test came from a number of sources, including Dan Bagley and the 1988 *Toronto Star* article by Damien Cox (cited in the Bibliography). Stories of Brian McKee come from Rick Prashaw and Mo McGuinty.

11. In the Land of Silver

The overall texture of this chapter comes from the numerous stories I have been told by Cobalt people over the years about Costello. The quote from Charles Peguy comes from the book *Dorothy Day: A Selection from Her Writings and Readings.* Carrie Chenier was interviewed by the author as part of a larger study on hardrock mining culture.

12. A Priest and the Sacraments

I am indebted to the stories collected by St. Alphonsus parish following the death of Father Costello. The story of Costello at the Parry Sound Orange Hall was told in the *Toronto Star* article by Ken Campbell. Details about Costello's attempts to work with single or widowed women came from the book of memories published by the parish following his death. The Father Costello joke about the rosary and the margarita was said at his 40th-anniversary celebration Mass. Information on the Copenhagen Old-Timers tournament came from the souvenir program supplied by the Landers family.

13. St. Martin of Schumacher

This information came through a number of interviews.

14. The Face of Christ

Much of the analysis I tried to provide on the gospel vision of serving the poor stems from the years I worked with my wife running a Catholic Worker house for the homeless in Toronto. In 1988, my wife and I visited with Father Costello and his housekeeper, Toni, and talked with them about the work with the marginalized. Information on personalism comes from the book *Breaking Bread*. The anonymous quote in this chapter comes from the book of memories published by St. Alphonsus parish following Costello's death. Costello's interest in G.K. Chesterton was mentioned by family members. His interest in Hans Küng was mentioned by Dan Bagley.

15. A World in Change

Ken Campbell's article appeared in the *Toronto Star* on April 9, 2000. Father Bill Scanlan's comments appeared in "Faith Revives with Humorous Touch," Frank Jones, *Toronto Star*, June 24, 1986. I relied on a number of newspaper articles – all cited in the Bibliography – for details around the Flying Fathers of this period. Analysis of John Paul II's impact on the Church came from reading a number of microfiche articles relating to the period after he was installed as pope, including "More Tolerance Wanted of Pope," AP Story, *Timmins Daily Press*, Oct. 1, 1980, and "Talks with Pope Said Significant," Canadian Press, *Timmins Daily Press*, November 19, 1980. The impact on the U.S. Catholic Church was marked by numbers compiled by the U.S. Bishops' National Review Board, which estimated that 4,392 clergy were involved in the abuse of 10,667 people. The context for the ever-tightening rules regarding sacraments and the resulting effects on the parishes have been covered by the author in a number of articles written for *Catholic New Times*.

16. Pulling the Goalie

This chapter is based on interviews cited in the Bibliography.

Bibliography

Books

Angus, Charlie and Louie Palu. *Mirrors of Stone: Fragments from the Porcupine Frontier.* Toronto: Between the Lines Press, 2001.

Chesterton, G.K. *The Common Man.* New York: Sheed and Ward, 1950.

Daly, Bernard. *Beyond Secrecy: The Untold Story of Canada and the Second Vatican Council.* Ottawa: Novalis, 2003.

Dawson, Christopher. *Religion and the Rise of Western Culture.* New York: Image Books, 1950.

Duplacey, James and Joseph Romain. *Images of Glory: The Toronto Maple Leafs.* Toronto: McGraw-Hill Ryerson, 1990.

Elliott, Lawrence. *I Will Be Called John: A Biography of Pope John XXIII.* New York: Reader's Digest Press/E.P. Dutton, 1973.

Gaudreau, Guy. "Les ouvriers-mineurs de Timmins (1915–1940): Les canadiens-français, mais surtout les autres." Lecture delivered to Laurentian University, 1988.

Girdwood, Charles, Lawrence Jones and George Lonn. *The Big Dome.* Toronto: Cybergraphics Company.

Graham, Frank. *Lou Gehrig: A Quiet Hero.* New York: G.P. Putnam and Sons, 1942.

Houston, Cecil, J. Smyth and J. William. *The Sash Canada Wore.* Toronto: University of Toronto Press, 1980.

Leonard, Elmore. *Touch.* New York: Arbor House, 1987.

Mackay, Donald. *The Lumberjacks.* Toronto: McGraw-Hill Ryerson, 1978.

McFarlane, Brian. *50 Years of Hockey, 1917–1967.* Toronto: Pagurian Press, 1967.

Miller, William. *All Is Grace: The Spirituality of Dorothy Day.* New York: Doubleday, 1987.

Piehl, Mel. *Breaking Bread: The Catholic Worker and the Origin of Catholic Radicalism in America.* Philadelphia: Temple University Press, 1982.

Quigley, Margaret and Michael Garvey. *The Dorothy Day Book: A Selection from her Writings and Readings*. Springfield, IL: Templegate Publishers, 1982.

Rice, Edward. *The Man in the Sycamore Tree: The Good Times and the Hard Life of Thomas Merton*. New York: Image Books, 1970.

Robert, Wayne. *A Miner's Life: Bob Miner and the Union Organizing in Timmins, Kirkland Lake and Sudbury*. Hamilton, ON: McMaster University Press, 1977.

Shea, Kevin. *Barilko: Without a Trace*. Toronto: Fenn, 2004.

Sheen, Fulton. *These Are the Sacraments*. New York: Hawthorn Books, 1962.

Solski, Mike and John Smaller. *Mine Mill: The History of the International Union of Mine, Mill and Smelter Workers in Canada Since 1895*. Ottawa: Steel Rail Publishing, 1985.

Stone, Philip. *The 1948 Hockey Album*. Toronto: Canadian Sports Digest, 1948.

Stortroen, Magne. *An Immigrant's Journal*. Cobalt, ON: Highway Book Shop, 1982.

Van Paassen, Pierre. *To Number Our Days*. New York: Scribner and Sons, 1964.

Vasiliadis, Peter. *Dangerous Truth: Interethnic Competition in a Northeastern Ontario Gold Mining Community*. Doctoral Thesis. Simon Fraser University, British Columbia. December 1984.

Other Publications

Copenhagan 78: 3rd Annual Old Timers International Hockey Tournament. Souvenir Program. Danish Ice Hockey Union, 1978.

Flying Fathers Souvenir Program. November 2001.

The Flying Fathers. Humbert, Greg. Flying Fathers Inc., 1969.

In Loving Memory of Father Les Costello: A Collection of Thoughts, Memories, Poetry and More. St. Alphonsus Parish, 2003.

St. Martin de Porres. Dominican Saints of the Rosary Series. St. Martin de Porres Apostolate, Dublin Ireland. [no date]

The Tradition Lives On: The St. Mike's Majors. St. Michael's College School, 1998.

Newspaper and Magazine Articles

"Beloved Priest's Life Comes Full Circle." Kate Harries. *Toronto Star*. December 17, 2002.

"Death of a Parish." Charlie Angus. *Catholic New Times*. October 6, 2002.

"Decline in Clergy Abuse Mirrors U.S. Trend." Agostino Catholic News Service. *Catholic Register*. March 21, 2004.

"Double Funeral Held for Cornish Friends." *Porcupine Advance*. February 16, 1928.

"Faith Revives with Humorous Touch." Frank Jones. *Toronto Star.* June 24, 1986.

"Father Costello Is Honoured at Roast." *Timmins Daily Press.* November 4, 1980.

"Father Les Won't Talk Hockey." Ken Campbell. *Toronto Star.* April 9, 2000.

"Flying Father Bagley a Boost to Team." *Toronto Star.* August 28, 1988.

"Flying Father Had Wings on His Feet." Jim Kernaghan. *London Free Press.* December 2002.

"Founder of Leafs Conn Smythe Dies at 85." CP. *Timmins Daily Press.* November 19, 1980.

"Impressive Funeral of Group of Finnish Men on Wednesday." *Porcupine Advance.* February 16, 1928.

"Küng: Pope Has 'Betrayed Second Vatican Council.'" AFP. Interview. Hamburg, Germany. May 16, 2000.

"Mass Meeting Addressed by Speakers in Six Languages." *Porcupine Advance.* February 15, 1928.

"Mighty Quinn Probes Dark World of Alcoholism." Jim Bawden. *Toronto Star.* February 16, 1986.

"More Tolerance Wanted of Pope." AP. *Timmins Daily Press*, October 1, 1980.

"Murray Costello Decides to Forsake Hockey Career." *Timmins Daily Press*, May 16, 1957.

"New Marriage Rules." Editorial. *Timmins Daily Press*, November 20, 1979.

"Pontiff Raps Birth Control at Chicago Mass." *Timmins Daily Press*, October 6, 1979.

"Pope Receives Strong Reaction Against Stand on Women Priests." AP. *Timmins Daily Press*, October 5, 1979.

"Primal Papal Duty to Be More Reforms." AP. *Timmins Daily Press*, October 17, 1979.

"Rev. Costello Is Ordained in Ceremony at South End," Doug McLellan. *Timmins Daily Press.* May 30, 1957.

"The Rinkmen: Outdoor Rinks in the Porcupine." Gregory Reynolds. *HighGrader Magazine*, March 2001.

"The Saint of Schumacher: Les Costello." Gregory Reynolds. *HighGrader Magazine*, January 2003.

"Searching for Bill Barilko." Austin Jelbert. *HighGrader Magazine*, Summer 1999.

"Stanley Cup Priest." Doug McLellan. *Timmins Daily Press.* May 31, 1957.

"Talks with Pope Said Significant." CP. *Timmins Daily Press.* November 19, 1980.

"Timmins Has Made Major Contribution to Pro Hockey Ranks." Vic Travis. *Timmins Daily Press.* April 28, 1979.

"What's Left After Hockey? Ask Hannigans." Milt Dunnell. *Toronto Star.* April 21, 1991.

Interviews conducted by the author

Pete Babando, October 25, 2003.

Billie (Connell) Babando, October 25, 2003.

Dan Bagley, March 6, 2004.

Len Bilodeau, August 27, 2003.

Father John Caswell, December 1, 2003.

Cliff Connolly, September 2003.

Murray Costello, December 10, 2003.

Pat Hannigan, November 9, 2003.

Rita (Costello) Hogan, August 28, 2003

Florence Kelly, January 4, 2004.

Colleen Landers, December 21, 2003.

Mike Landers, December 21, 2003.

Gord Lapierre, October 25, 2003.

Johnny McCormack, January 3, 2004.

Shirley McGarry, October 25, 2003.

Gus Mortson, December 20, 2003.

Father Des O'Connor, September 2003.

D'Arcy Quinn, October 25, 2003.

Frank Quinn, September 1, 1999.

Ted Schmidt, November 9, 2003.

Father M.J. Scully, January 9, 2004.

George Stefanic, August 26, 2003.

Frank Young, October 30, 2003.

Margo (Quinn) Young, September 26, 2003.

Related Interviews

John Campsall, October 9, 1974 (self-interview).

Carlo Cattarello Sr., March 27, 1998.

Carrie Chenier, February 2000.

Hamer Disher, June 1, 1974 (interviewed by M. Stortroen).

Dave McLaren, 1999.

Bob Miner, February 10, 1976 (interviewed by M. Stortroen).

Gus Mortson, January 1999